paula mcchesney & sandy peckinpah

passion by design

Re-Decorate Your Bedroom and Re-Invent Your Love Life

To Randy & Anita

Here's to living a life of Passion!

— In Joy!

Paula

Passion by Design, Re-Decorate Your Bedroom and Re-Invent Your Love Life
© Copyright 2010 Paula McChesney and Sandra Peckinpah
All rights reserved.

Life Design Publishing
Published and Printed in the United States of America

Eros and Psyche (Psyche Revived by the Kiss of Love)
Antonio Canova (1757-1822)
The Louvre
Photograph: Brooks McChesney

Author Photo, back cover: Sean Decker

Books are available at quantity discounts when used to promote products or services. For information, please e-mail: info@PassionByDesign.com

ISBN: 1-4392-5931-3
ISBN-13: 9781439259313

Self-Help, Interior Design, Relationships

We dedicate this book to you, our readers,
and to our sweethearts, (you know who you are...).

Love, sex and romance are evergreen; they have been around in one form or another since the beginning of time, and it is our fervent hope that they will continue to be around, in one form, or another, forever.

The *visual images* of how love, sex and romance are expressed are subject to the whims of fashion, social mores and world consciousness.

What people consider beautiful is ever changing. What we loved one year, is "out" the next. With this in mind, we have chosen to format this book for you in a new and exciting way.

We have made all visual images available to you on our website:
www.PassionByDesign.com

This allows us to continually provide you, dear reader, with current, dynamic, beautiful images that we hope will inspire and motivate you to a life of

Passion by Design.

InJoy!
Paula and Sandy

Visit www.PassionByDesign.com and sign up to be a part of
the Passion by Design Network™.

"To laugh often and love much…to appreciate beauty,
to find the best in others, to give one's self…this is to have succeeded."

- Ralph Waldo Emerson

TABLE OF CONTENTS

PART ONE...CREATING YOUR PASSIONATE LIFE

PART TWO...PASSION BY DESIGN, THE FANTASIES COME TO LIFE

PASSION AND DESIRE

CHAPTER ONE
Passion And Desire

Passion and desire can attract everything you want in life! Passion By Design, Re-Decorate Your Bedroom and Re-Invent Your Love Life, is a system for a way of life that we promise, will bring you more passion, more love, increased satisfaction with the *one* you love, <u>and</u> the bonus…a gorgeous bedroom! We'll be guiding you in creating a romantic environment that sets the stage for love.

How did this book begin? Desire…purely desire. We wanted to know what it took to sustain a loving, romantic, vibrantly exciting love life. We wanted to find the magical equation that would bring passionate direction in our lives! We set out to discover:

- what makes relationships work,
- how to have passion and romance be the driving force in our relationships,
- how to sustain passionate sex and long-term intimacy,
- how to create the most drop dead gorgeous bedroom where all our fantasies can come true!

We all know that relationships are works in progress, constantly growing and changing. They can grow together, and they can grow apart. Life can throw interesting twists and challenges. Often, our relationship can be the only certain thing in our lives. It's important to treat that union with love, respect, and attention. Relationships can grow stale if it stays the same. Keep it vibrant and alive with lots of attention! Where you put your focus, is what your relationship will become.

The changing of your environment—your bedroom—should *also* be a work in progress; otherwise it would be as boring as eating the same thing every day! Our bedrooms, the lair for our love, <u>and</u> our sex lives, can benefit from constant change, just as the changing seasons freshens our outside domain.

Passion by Design is a fusion of your love life with its environment.

Within the pages of this book, you will discover:
- How to attract more intimacy, passionate lovemaking, and fun…within a stronger, more fulfilling relationship.
- How to design and set the Stage for love…get out the fireworks!
- How to be an enticing enchantress.
- The key to having a better relationship with improved communication skills.
- The art and techniques to being a "satisfied" woman by feeling confident with your feminine powers and getting everything you want from the man you love.

Guess What? There's a wild woman in you, just waiting to get out! Enjoy the pursuit!

Your Passion Notes

HOT MOROCCAN NIGHTS

CHAPTER TWO
Hot Moroccan Nights

This afternoon, you call him at work and tell him to meet you in the bedroom at 8:00. A night he will always remember awaits. You tell him to follow instructions you've left in a note on the front door.

He can hardly wait to leave. It's all he can think about. He checks his watch repeatedly. His anticipation works him into a passionate frenzy. He doesn't know what to expect…this is not the typical "you." As he pulls into the driveway, he unbuttons his shirt collar, the car jerks to a stop. He's embarrassed and hopes the neighbors didn't notice.

He runs to the front door and sees an envelope taped to it…my God… it's just as she promised. He grabs it off the door and turns it over to see your lipstick imprint pressed to the seal. His hands quiver as he rips it open…inside, it reads:

"Darling…Go into the bedroom. Light all of the candles you can find. Pour yourself a glass of wine from the bedside table. Strip off your clothes, and toss them aside, along with the stresses of your day. Be prepared for a night of love and fantasy.

On the pillow you will find a Genie bottle. Make a wish, and then open the bottle. Inside, it is filled with love potion…Kama Sutra Powder. Dust your manliness with the powder…and wait for me.

By the time he flings open the bedroom door, his shirt is off, he's hopping on one leg trying to get his pants off while in motion. He's eager to experience the promise of pleasures to come.

The music "Scheherazade" fills the room and the light scent of musky candles sets the mood. You glide through the Indian silk-draped doorway of your bedroom. You're an exotic vision wrapped in a gown of gossamer gauze. He sees the most beautiful woman he has ever known. The candles flicker, making your body look soft, and alluring as you slowly, teasingly walk toward him…, slowly, sensually … in bare feet with a Gypsy coin ankle bracelet, reminiscent of belly dancers in the palaces of Morocco.

Your man is propped up on one arm, watching your every move. He wears a broad smile and his body responds to your love dance. In his mind's eye, you have changed from your everyday personae to the woman he is powerless to re-sist. Your sultry eyes hold the promise of secrets yet to be revealed.

The sheer drape hugging your lovely curves falls gently away from your bo-som. Your skin glistens, your cheeks are flushed, and your décolleté heaves with passion. You slowly ease up onto the bed. You brush his lips with your own. Your mouth becomes the tool of his pleasure. Your man is now out of this world and into the physical plane of ecstasy…and you have done it. You are the woman of all his sexual fantasies yet to come.

Do you think this is only possible in the movies? Absolutely not! The can-dles were purchased from a grocery store for $4.99 each. Your gossamer gauze gown is actually a tablecloth taken from your linen closet down the hall. The In-dian silk fabric draping your doorway is a leftover bedspread from college days. Your skin glistens with shimmery body lotion from the local drug store. The anklet is the charm bracelet you've had in your jewelry box for years (a paper clip makes it long enough for your ankle). The Genie Bottle was snatched out of a child's magic set, and the Kama Sutra Powder is actually powdered sugar (makes it more tasty for you). But the technique with your tongue is all your own! Shall we go on with the fantasy or are you creating your own at this point?

It's up to him to discover your hidden secrets, but it's up to you to have a creative supply of fantasies. A man thinks about having sex every single day. On the Moroccan night alone, you have given him a whole new playground of sexual thoughts about *you!*

---------------------------------------♥---------------------------------------

You instinctually knew how to create fantasy as a child. You can recall that ability as an adult. Remember, variety is the key. Keep your relationship vibrant and alive by creating new fantasies!

That's the mini fantasy version of Hot Moroccan Nights. Did it make you laugh? We hope so.

Let's consider actually giving your bedroom a complete renovation, as though you are taking an extended vacation to Morocco…or anywhere else you choose! In the pages that follow, you'll learn everything you need to know for awakening a whole new dimension to your relationship set against the backdrop of an exciting new bedroom. It's "inspired design," not "theme design." It's a framework for you to create a room for renewed romance and arouse your relationship to new heights.

Let the pleasures begin!

Your Passion Notes

BRING VACATION SEX BACK HOME

A man travels the world over in search of what he needs, then returns home to find it.

- George Moore

CHAPTER THREE

Bring Vacation Sex Back Home

What is it about vacations? Faraway places offer couples an opportunity to detour out of the routine of their daily lives. Once again, the married couple can view each other as lovers, stripped of the rigidity and demands of every day life. It affords a change in venue, which stimulates the senses, and tickles the fantasies, and, travel brings out the sense of play in us.

Imagine the moment you are poolside in Hawaii and take that first sip of Mai Tai. It's the moment you let go, you feel the Trade Winds kissing your skin. Your lover looks relaxed and suddenly more appealing. He gazes at you with a flicker of sensual urgency in his eyes. After a few hours in the sun, your body is alive to every sensation. He takes your hand and lifts you from your reclining sun chaise and walks you toward the beach. The sand is warm between your toes. He drew you close, kisses you slowly…deeply. You feel the tingling excitement, beginning in the pit of your stomach. You are about to experience over-the-moon sensual delights…

Ahhhhh, if we could only take this moment back home.

Well…you can! By following the steps we outline in Passion By Design, you will learn how to bring that "vacation sex" back home and continue to have romantic vacation encounters, right there, in your own bedroom.

Here's what you can expect. We will guide you in mapping out a blueprint to create your romantic relationship and your gorgeous new bedroom. You will delight in your own private retreat where, as lovers, you can enjoy playing again, and again and again!

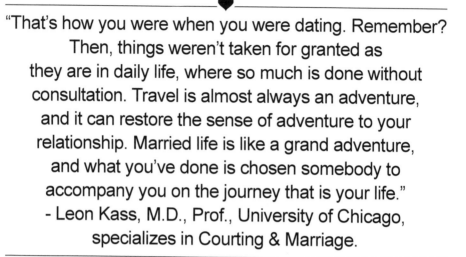

"That's how you were when you were dating. Remember?
Then, things weren't taken for granted as
they are in daily life, where so much is done without
consultation. Travel is almost always an adventure,
and it can restore the sense of adventure to your
relationship. Married life is like a grand adventure,
and what you've done is chosen somebody to
accompany you on the journey that is your life."
- Leon Kass, M.D., Prof., University of Chicago,
specializes in Courting & Marriage.

In the book, *How to Satisfy a Man Every Time...and have him beg for more!"* Noted author, Naura Hayden, conducted a surprising survey. She questioned 500 men of various ages. All were married, but the length of the marriages varied from 1 year to 57 years. Her results were so surprising; we felt it necessary to include them in our book.

When asked how often men would like to have sex, 94% replied they would like to have it *every* day! When asked if sex with their wives had gotten boring, 82% said *yes*.

Shocked? We were. This bolstered our commitment to developing techniques and strategies to sustain a long-term relationship to make <u>you</u> the focus of all <u>his</u> fantasies...and fulfill yours along the way!

"We've all heard, often enough, that men don't understand women, but I think it's much more universal that
women don't have a clue about the enormous importance of sexual excitement to men."
- Naura Hayden

It is *absolutely possible* to stimulate the senses, turn the heat on, and add new dimension to your sex life. You'll have fun doing it!

Let's take advantage of this powerful information to create new opportunities for satisfaction with our partners. Let's learn to be the object of our partner's sexual excitement.

There is so much joy to falling in love again...and staying in love. Follow the steps in *Passion By Design*, and you will re-awaken the enchantment in your relationship that first drew you together.

"Play, and you cease to be boring to one another. The tremendous advantage of travel is that you can play, and you have all day long to have fun. Think of the world as your playground, and break out of your everyday roles as spouse, parent, and target of telemarketers who call during dinner."
- Lenore Terr, M.D. UCSF author,
<u>Beyond Love and Work</u>

Your Passion Notes

DRAW YOUR RELATIONSHIP BLUEPRINT

Does the state of your bedroom parallel
the state of your relationship?

CHAPTER FOUR
Draw Your Relationship Blueprint

As an interior designer, Paula McChesney, ASID, creates lifestyles. Paula has had the opportunity to work with people on giving new direction to their homes' interiors. Interior design is not just creating beautiful furniture, window coverings, paint, and floors. It is a quest to marry function with comfort and beauty.

The first step is to map out the couple's routine, the entire twenty-four hours. She maps the course in their home: where they sit to have their morning coffee, the steps they take to get dressed for the day, the places they like to put their feet up, how they like to eat, and sleep, and more importantly—romance. She considers virtually every aspect of their lives in creating a new environment that brings joy, comfort, beauty, and harmony.

Paula asks her clients to peruse photographs of furniture, homes, and colors, to determine their likes and dislikes. The couple will usually demonstrate totally different visions! *She* may focus on romance and color. *He* may focus on comfort and ease. Paula evaluates the tastes of both people and sets out to create a style that complements the desires of both.

It takes an intuitive designer to create an environment that will address the wants, needs, and desires, of two distinctly different people. It's necessary to research the dynamics of their relationship and the common denominators that make it work.

Now here's the important step: she discreetly assesses the state of their relationship. Are they asking her to make changes in their environment out of inspiration or boredom? Is their ultimate goal to change their lives, by changing what they sit on, where they sleep, or the blinds they draw at night? Are they happy with each other, or are they subconsciously trying to find something to put spark back in their relationship? The state of the master bedroom often parallels the state of a couple's relationship. The physical environment often reflects the emotional environment of a couple's relationship.

Could <u>he</u> be hoping that a new bed would rev up his wife's desire for sex? Is <u>she</u> wishing that new lighting would make her look more attractive to her husband? Are they seeking passion that somehow got lost in the day-to-day business of life? It could be all of these and more. Finding their passion is key!

Passion is an emotion that is stimulated by sight, sound, touch, taste, and feel.

Paula's goal is to tap into the elements of design to stimulate passion! In design, these senses are an important consideration in the selection of color palettes, fabrics, furniture, window and wall coverings, and room configuration. By changing the design elements in the home, these senses <u>can</u> be re-awakened. Redesigning a couple's bedroom can bring the playful lovers of days gone by together in the bedroom, once again.

The way to keep passion alive is to consistently change our playground, not the players.

When sex in a relationship is fulfilling, it comprises one of the many important facets of a relationship. When sex is bad or non-existent in a marriage, that missing component becomes magnified and can quickly develop into a destructive dominating force in the partnership.

It's like standing on the shore, the waves slowly eroding the foundation around you; and yet, you are still standing. You may not even notice the erosion. Then, one big wave knocks you off balance, and you realize that your life has been washed out from under your feet. What happened to your foundation? It seemed so secure just a wave or two ago. The point is this… in order for a couple to sustain love; they have to constantly refresh the sand that has washed out from under their feet!

Men and woman ultimately want the same thing---to be loved.

However, men and women approach this need and desire in extremely different ways.

Your Passion Notes

THE SEASONS OF LOVE

♥

"I once had a rose named after me, and I was very flattered. But I was not pleased to read the description in the catalogue; no good in a bed, but fine up against a wall."

-Eleanor Roosevelt

CHAPTER FIVE
The Seasons of Love

You're about to go through the process of recognizing, awakening, and being present with your relationship. Enjoy the journey, as the cumulative experience is the core of your love. It's much like planting a garden. Planting the seeds fills you with the anticipation and vision of what's to come. The process of tending the garden: watering, fertilizing, tilling, and pruning, all contribute to the joy. You marvel as the garden blooms. Each process is magical. The bliss of seeing the garden in full bloom brings the promise that spring always comes again!

You are the attractor of what shows up in your life. You are the creator of your reality. Just as nature does its dance around the seasons, the human body reacts in the flush of attraction, the heat of arousal, the tremble of its muscles, and the exuberance of the emotion called passion. Reality has cycles just like the seasons of nature.

It's natural for relationships to go through seasons and cycles. Our hearts are as tender as the shoots of the young plant. As time passes we get our roots firmly planted in the relationship and become more confident and sometimes more complacent. With Passion by Design, you're just about to uproot that complacency.

If, one day, while tending your garden, you discovered a magical herb that had the power to make you more beautiful, keep you young at heart, bring vibrancy and health to your body, and sustain your marriage into the happily ever after; however, you must take this herb on a regular basis or it's power would fail you...would you take that herb? Yes?

Well, here is your magic herb.

It's........................

.........Sex

It's a bit of a trick answer because we are using sex in its broadest form. It encompasses so much more than the word we have come to know. Sex is a form of intimacy that includes physical and emotional harmony.

Sexual drive is a desire for closeness in sharing our lives and our environment with another being. It surpasses lust that is merely a physical urge. True intimacy is a coupling of a sexual foundation with love, honesty, caring, enjoyment, and emotional fulfillment.

Sex is the way that a man connects romantically with a woman. Romance is the way that a woman connects sexually with a man.

Next question.

Think of your favorite dinner. What if the law said you must choose your favorite dinner, and you must eat <u>this</u>, and <u>only</u> this dinner for the rest of your life. How do you think you would feel about this dinner? Three years from now? Ten years from now? Twenty-five years from now?

Would it still be your favorite dinner? We don't think so. The message we'd like to hit home, is this:

Sex is a necessary ingredient to maintain a healthy romantic relationship… and variety within the relationship is the spice that keeps it fresh and desirable.

What if we applied the principles used in re-designing a bedroom to re-designing one's love life? At the very core of love is one's self.

You would never set out to build a home without a set of blueprints, leaving the result to be haphazardly determined. Yet we spend less time and conscious thought on the designing and building of our most intimate relationship.

Everything you do is a choice in building the framework of what your relationship is...the good and the bad. Within the pages of this Passion System, we offer you a way to look at the structure of your relationship, and to redesign the parts of the relationship that aren't working, and strengthen the parts that are.

Do you experience times when you absolutely love and adore the one you're with, and other times, you don't want to be in the same room?

These are cycles that happen naturally. The resilient rose is cut back every winter, leaving just brown twigs sticking out from the ground. In its cycle of life, it begins to sprout new leaves, tender and green and goes on to bloom gloriously spring after spring.

Within the pages of Passion by Design, you'll learn how to weather the storms, shorten the cycles of brown twigs and thorns...and enhance the blooms of your love.

Your Passion Notes

YOUR RELATIONSHIP 101...PASSION QUIZ

"I have found men who didn't know how to kiss.
I've always found time to teach them."

-Mae West, actress

CHAPTER SIX
Your Relationship 101...Passion Quiz

As we embark on this love journey, we encourage you to create a group of close women friends to share your *Passion By Design* journey. Allow them the joy of re-writing their own relationships as you re-write yours.

Human beings draw energy from each other. Sex is not necessarily something that is easily and openly discussed. Discussed through the common goal of re-designing a bedroom, and it might be a bit more approachable. The more comfortable we become in discussing sex, love, and romance, the more avenues we open to becoming sensual, sexual beings without emotional or societal barriers.

In forming a *Passion by Design* group (visit www.PassionByDesign.com), you can expand the potential, reap the benefits of feedback, learn from your friends' inspired ideas and experiences, not to mention the possibility that a member of your group may just have that crystal bedside lamp you need to complete your new boudoir!

We're about to explore our favorite subject...ourselves. The first exercise in our system for re-shaping your love life is a fun and titillating quiz. It will give you insight into the current state of your romantic relationship. Get a pencil and let the quiz begin!

PASSION QUIZ

Circle the letter that is most like your relationship, today.

1) When did you last change the furnishings in your bedroom?
   a) Recently
   b) 3 years ago.
   c) 4-15 years ago.
   d) 15-? years ago.

2) You would describe your sex life as
   a) Romantic and adventurous
   b) Routine
   c) Needing a little kick start

3) Your bedroom is
   a) Beautiful and a pleasure to be in
   b) Only okay, same old, same old
   c) Difficult and needs work

4) Making love with your lover usually involves
   a) One favorite position and location
   b) A couple of sure fire positions
   c) A number of different positions and locations

5) When you are in public with your partner
   a) You hold hands
   b) Hesitate to show affection
   c) Are spontaneous with kisses and other signs of affection

6) When you and your mate kiss you,
   a) Still feel that spark
   b) Feel nothing
   c) Feel safe and content

7) When you argue with your lover
   a) It's resolved quickly to get it out of the way
   b) It lasts for days
   c) Argue until you reach a satisfying compromise

8) In bed, you typically wear
   a)   A nightgown, tee shirt and shorts, or pajamas
   b)   A sexy negligee
   c)   Something you know your lover thinks is cute on you
   d)   Nothing at all

9) The state of my marriage/relationship is:
   a)   Passionate, adventurous.
   b)   Happy, comfortable, but could benefit from a new spark.
   c)   Boring.

10) How often do you praise or compliment the one you love?
   a)   Every day
   b)   2-3 times a week
   c)   A couple times a month or less
   d)   It's been so long, I can't remember when

11) How was sex on your last vacation together?
   a)   Mind blowing, extremely satisfying.
   b)   Satisfying, pleasant.
   c)   Disappointing or didn't happen

12) How much thought went into love making in planning your vacation?
   a)   The focal point, including the purchase of new lingerie.
   b)   A passing thought, but restaurants/shopping were important, too.
   c)   Didn't cross your mind.

13) What happened when you arrived home from your vacation?
   a)   The romance and sex continued.
   b)   The passion lasted for a few days...maybe a few weeks.
   c)   Nothing changed when we got back to our old routine.

14) Does your appearance affect your feelings about having sex?
   a)   I'm not an attractive person
   b)   Yes, I'm not attractive enough to be desired, I need to lose 10 lbs.
   c)   Some days I feel sexy, other times I don't
   d)   I'm extremely desirable just the way I am.

Quiz, Continued

15) How much time do you and you partner spend making your bedroom beautiful?
   a) Add or move things seasonably
   b) Ignore for the most part
   c) Make changes regularly, even if only fresh flowers
   d) Have not even noticed how it looks for years

16) How often do you surprise you lover with something out of the ordinary… an unexpected date, a special dinner, a gift, a new toy?
   a) Sometimes
   b) Hardly ever
   c) Often
   d) All the time

17) How often does your lover surprise you with something special?
   a) Sometimes
   b) Never
   c) Often
   d) All the time

18) In your relationship, you
   a) Tend to take your partner for granted
   b) Look forward to being with your partner and make time for it
   c) Go through stages of being passionately in love, other times you're just good companions
   d) Try your best to make romance and love the focus of your relationship on an ongoing basis

19) When your lover wants to try something new in bed, you
   a) Are nervous but go along with it
   b) Look forward to it…anything goes
   c) Refuse, but offer him something else
   d) Say no, and hope that it doesn't offend him
   e) Are outraged, even angry with him

20) How often do you think about your lover in a romantic way, throughout the day?
 a) Sometimes
 b) Rarely
 c) Often
 d) All the time, it's never far from your thoughts

21) You and your mate's communication is
 a) Usually good
 b) Open and clear
 c) Sometimes obstructed by outside influences
 d) Not clear, needs work

22) In decorating your home
 a) You make all the decisions and he goes along with it
 b) He makes all the decisions and you go along with it
 c) You usually make decisions together
 d) Love to design and shop together for your home
 e) It's the joining of your things when you became a couple

23) Your children
 a) Always knock before entering your bedroom
 b) Are informed that Mom and Dad need their "love and quiet time"
 c) Barge in without warning (where's the lock!)
 d) Sleep with you
 e) Do not have children, does not apply

24) When you make love, you
 a) Are quiet, but the sex is good
 b) Are comfortable making passionate sounds
 c) Scream with delight at the point of no return (the big "O")
 d) Stifle any and all love making noises

25) You believe
 a) That the key to a long lasting relationship is love, sex, and romance
 b) That love is a commitment that needs constant attention
 c) There's no such thing as forever romance and sexual excitement

SCORING

Question	a	b	c	d	e	Your score
1	3	2	1	0		
2	3	2	1			
3	2	3	2			
4	1	2	3			
5	2	1	3			
6	3	0	2			
7	1	1	3			
8	1	3	2	3		
9	3	2	1			
10	3	2	1	0		
11	3	2	1			
12	3	2	1	0		
13	3	1	0			
14	0	1	2	3		
15	2	1	3	0		
16	2	0	3	3		
17	2	0	3	3		
18	1	3	2	3		
19	2	3	1	1	0	
20	2	1	3	3		
21	2	3	1	1		
22	1	1	3	3	0	
23	2	3	0	0	0	
24	1	3	4	0		
25	4	3	0			
—	—	—	—	—	—	Total:

REPORT CARD

Score 0-34

We're really ecstatic you bought this book *just in time*. Your relationship is ready for a new and exciting beginning. In the next several chapters, we're going to offer new and exciting ways to turn on the passion and add some spice. Relationships take a lot of care and thought to keep the spark glowing. The first step in doing so is to up your own personal sex quotient. The rest is sure to follow by carefully doing the steps and projects we suggest in the book.

Immediately on your "must do list" is to go out and purchase some sexy new bras, underwear, and other lingerie. Tonight, greet him with a candle light dinner (children should be tucked into bed early), wearing your new lingerie underneath a new seductive robe. Don't forget to leave a message on his voicemail. Tell him you are planning something special...make a specific time for him to be home, and tell him you are in the mood for love. This will get his thoughts racing...and be prepared, for he just might arrive home a little early!

You may be at the bottom of the grading score; you are definitely on top of the situation! Good for you! You have so much to look forward to!

Score 35-59

Your relationship is on track and ready to go the distance with a tweak now and then. Congratulations, you bought this book to promote enhance the passion that already exists. The flames could be fanned a bit, and the fire could use some more kindling, but in the next several chapters, you will learn ways to turn that campfire into a red-hot bonfire! Your communication is good and things are comfortable without being boring. You find your sex life is improved with vacations, and other changes and variations. You are ready and willing. Often, the only thing stopping you is finding your time together being compromised by daily life. You are about to learn how to bring that passion into your home, full time. Immediately on your must do list...buy some new towels and bedding, bath oils, massage oil, candles, and a good bottle of wine or champagne. Make an appointment with your mate this evening to experience a candle lit bath together, or tell him you have a very special massage in mind. Serve dinner in your bedroom and play some Barry White music. Spend the time tonight, telling him how much you appreciate him in your life and that you find him even sexier today than when you first met him. You have such potential for an extremely satisfying, long lasting relationship!

Score 60 and Above

Wow! There aren't many out there like you! You must have an extremely wonderful man in your life, and he must feel equally fortunate to have you. More than likely, you bought this book to enhance and improve on the sizzle and spice you already have. You are ready for some ideas to redecorate your love boudoir to continue your quest for a relationship that lasts over time and re-ignites itself with the passion you share with each other. Within the pages of this book, we have some new and sensual ideas for your relationship, your sex life, and your bedroom…and you may have some ideas for us! Onward!

Immediately on your "must do list:" Go to your local music store and buy some music CDs that means something special to both of you. Perhaps it's a movie score from your favorite movie you saw together, a special concert, a Broadway play, or a CD of an artist you both love. Call him at work and tell him you're putting together a new soundtrack…your own soundtrack of your romantic life together.

Go to your garden and snip roses, or buy some from your florist (ask for those that are no longer as fresh and you might find the price goes down). Pull back your bedding and sprinkle rose petals on the bed. Have you ever experienced the softness of rose petals on naked skin? Light oodles of candles, chill a bottle of your favorite wine, put together a platter of food you can nibble with your fingers, and then…make sweet, sensuous love, all night long. We'll get back to you tomorrow!

Your Passion Notes

FANTASY & LAUGHTER...THE KEYS
TO INTIMACY

"The most wasted day is that in which
we have not laughed."

-Chamfort

CHAPTER SEVEN
Fantasy & Laughter. . . The Keys
To Intimacy

The core of any successful relationship is intimacy; Webster's College Dictionary defines *intimacy* as "a close and affectionate personal relationship." Intimacy can be experienced among family, friends, or lovers. Intimacy shows itself in the way we are with each other and is a reflection of who we believe ourselves to be. What you want to put forward in an intimate relationship is honest, loving, and true. Couples have the ability to add a dimension of intimacy that they share with no other. . .physical intimacy.

Lucky us. . .sex is the bonus of a loving relationship that has the ability to set our world on fire. . .in the beginning.

Let's think back even further in time, when sex was the driving force in establishing your relationship as an "intimate couple". . .to the moment that you *knew* you were in love. It was a love that could not be denied. . .full of passion, possibility, and romance. You felt that you had met the man of your dreams. . . the man that you wanted to be with for the rest of your life.

It's time to look for ways to make your love NEW again! Fantasy and laughter are the keys.

Your world suddenly turned into "Somewhere Over the Rainbow." Everything you saw, heard, touched, tasted, and felt was more beautiful through the eyes of new love. Flowers came in colors you never realized existed! Food had never tasted so good. Music was sweeter and lyrics were written just for you and the one you love. Touch had a magic all of its own, sending shivers of bliss throughout your body. Everything, including your heart, was achingly alive.

Remember back when you couldn't keep your hands off of each other... when holding hands during a walk in the park set your body on fire! Every stoplight meant a moment to kiss deeply until a car behind you honked impatiently at the green light. Remember when 60 seconds in an elevator meant 60 seconds of "over the moon," but risky, passion?

By the time you and your lover found the bedroom, the heat sent you both into a state of ecstasy that launched your dreams and fantasies of sharing a life together.

"The meeting of two personalities is like the contact of two chemical substances: if there is any reaction, both are transformed."
- Carl Jung

In the beginning, designing a life together was a journey filled with exhilaration and expectation, because every part of it was new. You had planned on living the rest of your life as lovers. You pulled together a home that reflected where you were in that station of life. Your sex life needed no encouragement because it was a force so strong, you both believed the lust would never end.

Now you are a few years down the road. Your history together has given you the gift of a terrific friendship, shared memories, and possibly a few children. Chances are, if you're like most of us, you've settled into a predictable routine.

Although you are happy, and still together, you are housed in an environment that hasn't changed much over the years. Your home is filled with the same taste and furniture choices you had made in the beginning...and it may not be quite as exciting as it once was. Possibly, your sex life reflects the same state of affairs.

Life is good, but there are times when you long for the magic. Are you secretly afraid you have lost your desire for your partner? Are you afraid he has lost his desire for you? The last time you made love with wild abandon was last spring on your vacation to Hawaii. Making love in your bedroom with the same four-poster bed, the matching bedside tables with the matching bedside lamps, which match "his" and "hers" dressers, doesn't quite inspire the same kind of passion. What's happened to that spark?

Don't worry…you're not alone. Couples everywhere are susceptible to the "daily life flu."

It's a bug that grows slowly in a relationship with the added pressures of daily life. Its symptoms are sexual lethargy, physical boredom, and hidden frustration. It infiltrates relationships usually sometime after the first year or two, and destroys the way we were…wasn't there a Barbra Streisand song about that very thing?

How do you create a new level of intimacy: titillating, sexy, sensual… and irresistible?

The secret ingredients of intimacy that people often for get are fantasy and laughter set against the backdrop of a stimulating and beautiful bedroom environment.

Fantasy is fun! Fantasy is the power of suggestion. It's an opportunity to play! It's about being someone or something you have always wanted to be! And most importantly, it's a vital ingredient in shaping your beliefs that you *can* achieve and create everything you choose to be, do and have.

We remind you of the power within us to create our own destiny, and the role that the Law of Attraction has in our lives. Visualizing and attracting the relationship you choose to have is one step closer to having it.

Remember what we said about variety in one's relationship? It is the ingredient that never gets old. When your relationship began, it was the "newness" and the "unexpectedness" that gave it the fuel for passion. You couldn't wait to discover one more thing about your lover…and he couldn't wait to discover one more thing about you!

Laughter is a SEXY ingredient of long-term relationships. Laughter stimulates the "happiness endorphins" in the body! When those endorphins are released, your skin glows, your body senses are heightened, your brain works more efficiently, and you feel GREAT! It's as simple as that. There's nothing sexier than a woman whose endorphins have come out of hibernation!

The key to finding the laughter is making the bedroom a fun place to be…. and using fantasy. Remember our Moroccan fantasy? We're going to show you how to do that and more…you're going to have so much fun!

Your Passion Notes

WISH AND FANTASY JOURNAL

"Nothing risqué, nothing gained."

-Alexander Woolcott

CHAPTER EIGHT
Wish And Fantasy Journal

You have many wishes and fantasy options for your love life and a brand new bedroom! Start a journal of notes in a *Passion Notebook*™ This can be a three-ring notebook in a color you love. Buy a few sets of colorful dividers with pockets and some paper. It's important to use color in this notebook, for we are awakening and stimulating our imagination and our senses! You will continue to add to this notebook in the next several chapters. Most important is an evaluation of the state of your bedroom, your relationship, and your sex life. Making your wishes and fantasies come true is what this book is all about. It's an adventure we're sure you'll enjoy...

Having trouble identifying your romantic fantasies? The best way to become the most desirable woman on earth is to begin by setting the stage. Think like an actress studying for a role. An actress uses her past experiences and senses to create her character! She recalls things in her life that parallel the feelings of the character she is portraying. This is easy for you because you already know there was a sexual past that felt lust and desire.

Fantasies are Pleasure Mediations

It's amazing how the written word can have such power in bringing our dreams to fruition. One year from now, you may look at this list and be quite surprised at how many of your wishes have come true. Perhaps there really is a genie in a bottle out there somewhere!

Now don't wait a second longer...do it quickly so that you write the first impulse that comes to mind.

Example: I wish... *I could make love in Paris.*

Now begin to dream of all your wishes!

ROMANTIC WISH & FANTASY JOURNAL

I wish...

I wish...

I wish...

I wish...

I wish...

fantasy...

fantasy...

fantasy...

Now from *your* Wish and Fantasy Journal, you're going to create your own personal romantic fantasies!

Close your eyes and become that person your lover first met. Feel the flutter in your stomach when you used to look at him. Soften your lips, your eyes, and your body language. Your body is beautiful. Make peace with it by playing the role of the sexiest woman alive! Your man finds you irresistible.

Leave no room for being self-conscious. One full figured beauty said it best: "When I'm the only naked woman in the room, my body is worth a million bucks to him!"

Where are you when your eyes are closed? Is it your own bedroom or has your mind set the stage? Let your mind drift to a place that is romantic to you. It could be a bedroom you've seen in magazines, a room you vacationed in on the island of Fiji, a room out of a romance novel you might have read, or a place yet to be created in real life. Picture it in detail, for we're going to incorporate these places into the design of your bedroom <u>and</u> your sex life.

Do you hear music? Is it Barry White or Andrea Boccelli? Perhaps you're in a luxurious hotel and the sound track from "Somewhere in Time" evokes chords of passion. Mentally catalogue the music that first comes to mind, for this will be your *"Passion Soundtrack"* for your new romantic life.

Which colors are you visualizing right now? Wrap yourself in the color. Think of it as soft silk velvet that kisses every part of your body it touches. Is it a color that flatters you? Even if you won't be wearing the colors you choose… it <u>is</u> your backdrop for your fantasy. It's important that it's a color that enhances your own beauty. What colors make you feel beautiful?

Allow yourself to play act the entire romantic encounter. Your lover now enters the stage. See yourself, as you want him to see you. Feel yourself. You move gently to the rhythm of your body. You are the sexiest, most desirable woman alive.

Your Passion Notes

PASSION VISION BOARD

"Man's desires are limited by his perceptions;
none can desire what he has not perceived."

-William Blake

CHAPTER NINE
Passion Vision Board

This is fun... You're going to create a Passion Vision Board™, which is a visual picture of your dreams and desires. This is a tried and true tool of many motivational systems to align your conscious mind with your subconscious mind and the energy of the universe.

Get several magazines and newspapers and cut out pictures of anything and everything that makes you feel playful and sexy. ...anything you desire in your life, your perfect home, the bedroom you desire, travel, your perfect body... anything. This is for your eyes only. Be as outrageous as you choose.

Use a glue stick to paste these pictures onto a poster board. You're going to put this somewhere private, perhaps inside a cupboard, a closet, wherever you choose. Look at this each and every day. Admire it. It's a tool to making your desires a reality.

Your Passion Notes

GAMES AND TOYS KEEP FANTASY ALIVE!

♥

"There are a number of mechanical devices
which increase sexual arousal, particularly
in women. One is the Mercedes-Benz
380 SL Convertible."

-P.J. O'Rourke

CHAPTER TEN
Games And Toys Keep Fantasy Alive!

Let's consider the importance of games and toys in people's lives. Surely you've noticed how games keep children occupied and stimulated.

♥

Remember to always keep your "child heart"... Especially when it comes to romance!

The two of you are both grown-up children and still looking for that sense of fun and adventure, and who wouldn't want to continue to have fun!

If you're a mother, you put a huge amount of effort into entertaining and providing toys and games to keep your children from being bored. Do you think your husband or mate is any different...NO! We propose applying some of the same principles and efforts directed toward your adored man to keep him entertained and interested in YOU!

♥

Remember... boredom is the number one relationship killer. You're about to change that!

Toys have come a long way in the last several decades. Sex shops are no longer just for the man. Surely you've heard about the fun and innovative lingerie and adult toy parties. They're like a Tupperware Party for sex and romance! If you have the opportunity...attend one of these parties, or you might even consider giving the party for your Passion Group of women!

Another option is to go online and look for websites that cater to women. Stay with your level of comfort. The Internet can be full of unwelcome surprises. Use it with caution.

Pay attention, take notes, and buy toys. We guarantee you'll learn things you didn't know! The woman's vibrator, for instance, has come a long way since the one that masks as a muscle relaxer. Now they have vibrators that look like various body parts, even discreet vibrators that can fit between the two of you so that you can be stimulated on the outside, while he's inside of you.

One important note we'd like to make: if you have children or a housekeeper, consider putting a lock on your bedside drawer where you keep all of these toys, or purchase your very own toy chest with a lock! Be clear, this is not dirty or shameful…it's simply private.

♥

A Word about the Children

Even though you love your children, there should be some guidelines regarding their time in your bedroom. We feel it is important to make rules for the children (knocking, for instance), regarding their entrance to your private room. This room is not their playground. This is your and your husband's sacred sanctuary… where <u>you</u> play out your fantasies!

Bubble baths are also a form of sensuous play. They feel good against the skin, and if your bath is large enough for the two of you…it's foreplay! Scented bubbles tease and tantalize the sense of smell. Have a bowl of chocolates beside the bath to tempt and titillate the taste buds.

Try having a bath ready for him when he gets home. Light candles, play music, and serve his favorite drink as you scrub his back, rub his feet, and massage his shoulders.

Wear a daring negligee while you offer your services. By the time he gets out of the bath, he'll be ready to romp…right into making love.

Toys are fun! Toys are fantasy! Toys can enhance your sexual play!

Your Passion Notes

COLOR YOUR WAY TO PASSION

"The whole world, as we experience it visually, comes to us through the mystic realm of color."

-Hans Hofmann, artist

CHAPTER ELEVEN
Color Your Way To Passion

Many people feel they don't have "decorating talent." This is a misconception we intend to alter. Treat yourself to a latté and a day at the bookstore. You can gain a simple education in style by perusing decorating magazines and interior design books. Start noticing the design style that appeals to you. Purchase the ones that excite you.

In your Passion Notebook, divide the sections into the following categories:

- Fantasy Bedrooms
- Wall Colors
- Fabrics
- Furniture Pieces
- Vacation Inspirations
- Romantic Personal Memories
- Break Outside the Box
- Color Palette Worksheets
- Change List

Gather the pictures of the bedroom styles that appeal to you. Start pulling pictures from magazines, photocopy pictures from books, and look through online and mail order catalogues. Put the pictures into your *Passion Notebook*™.

Look through travel books and magazines. Look at vivid pictures of vacation spots that appeal to you. These can be fantasy places, places you've always dreamed of, or places you've actually been...places which hold a sexual, sensual appeal, places that increase your sexual appetite. Snip out pictures of the places that you might want to re-create.

Go to your own photo albums and select photographs that have happy and romantic memories for you.

The "Break Outside the Box" section in your notebook should include selections that are not within your current decorating style, but for some reason, sparks something in you. The object here is to break outside the box…to see things with new eyes. It could be pictures of a metropolitan apartment in New York, decorated exclusively in black, white and red. It could be a cozy cottage in England. This section is an opportunity to shape your likes and dislikes. Study the pictures to find out what it is that caught your eye.

Do the metropolitan apartment pictures evoke a cold, untouchable feeling or does it evoke a sleek sexy desire? Does the cozy cottage make you feel claustrophobic? These are feelings to take note of when decorating your own environment.

Don't limit yourself to bedrooms you feel you can afford or are typically "you." We want you to expand your thinking and your desires. That which you think actually attracts the means to achieve it.

With the *Passion By Design System™*, we are helping you create opportunities for your romantic future. Keep up with new ideas and trends when you see them. Add them to your book. Fashion and style constantly changes and offers us opportunities for new self-expression.

It's all about constant change and new stimulation. Down the road, you'll refer to this book and create a new bedroom when the current bedroom no longer suits today's "fantasy."

♥

Money is no object right now. Why? Because we're designing your personal Passion Style™, and at this moment, it's your fantasy creation.

Your Passion Notes

PASSION PALETTE™ WORKSHEET

"At moments of great enthusiasm it seems to me that no one in the world has ever made something this beautiful and important."

-M.C. Escher, artist

CHAPTER TWELVE
Passion Palette™ *Worksheet*

Find a color wheel and look at colors with an emotional "eye." What colors appear warm and inviting? Which seem cold and uninviting? Are some colors more playful than others are? Do you feel happy when you look at certain colors, and sad when you look at others?

Divide a piece of paper into columns or photocopy the chart on the next page. Put this in the color section of your notebook.

Take a walk with Mother Nature. Notice color combinations in flowers. Note the unexpected, like bright pink gerbera daisies nestled next to orange poppies. Blue hyacinths tucked next to crimson roses and purple snapdragons. It's amazing how everything seems to work in nature!

Think carefully about colors that evoke different feelings of happiness, playfulness, joy, arousal, sexy, free spirited, even sadness. Perhaps the color red represents a sexy bra and under panties. Green evokes the memory of the lush greenery that surrounded your hotel in Hawaii. Orange and pink may bring the feelings of serenity when you watched a spectacular sunset with your lover.

If dark blue is the color of the dress you wore to dinner the night you and your husband had the worst fight of your marriage, list it in the sad, unhappy column. Remember that dark blue dress? Is dark blue also the color of your bedspread? How does that color make you feel?

Take your time with this exercise, savor the experience of exploration, and pay attention to the *first* emotion you feel when you look at a color, for that impulse is the true feeling you have.

PASSION PALETTE™ WORKSHEET

Describe the colors that make you feel:

Happy, Joyful	Beautiful	Roman-tic Sensual	Hot, Sexy Passionate	Playful, On a Vacation	Sad Melancholy Unhappy
Example Salmon, Sunshine Yellow Periwinkle	Example Sunset Red Coral Forest Green	Example White Lace Lilac	Example "Night on the town Red" Black	Example Aquamarine Lime	Example Gray Beige

Here's a game for the two of you. Ask your lover about his opinion of color.

Make a game of naming a color, and tell him to say the first emotion that comes to mind. Will he think it's a silly game? Perhaps…but try to make it a playful game, with rewards, such as passionate kissing for five minutes if one of his colors falls in the same category. You could tempt him with oral delights if five of his colors match up in the same columns as yours.

There is more than one way to stimulate his sense memories. He may need a little visual help. Bring out the pictures of your trip to Hawaii, reminding him of the sunset you shared together. Remind him of the color of your wedding negligee.

After you've experienced the pleasure of rewarding your man for playing your game, make a list of the colors that you both agreed upon as being the colors that represent your relationship.

This is your Personal Passion Palette and we'll use it to re-create your environment. These are your colors...the colors that will pull you into the beginning of a new life together.

Your Passion Notes

EXISTING PASSION PALETTE WORK SHEET

"On the floor I am more at ease. I feel nearer, more a part of the painting, since this way I can walk around it, work from the four sides and literally be in the painting."

-Jackson Pollock, artist

CHAPTER THIRTEEN
Existing Passion Palette Work Sheet

We didn't say this was going to be easy! Stay committed to your goal…a romantic, sexy, fun filled, satisfying relationship for the rest of your life!

List the colors presently in your home…particularly your bedroom. Examine each room with a discerning eye. Don't edit yourself. This is an important evaluation tool.

Describe the colors that you currently have in your home:

Master Bedroom	Master Bath	Kitchen	Family Room	Living Room	Dining Room

Your Passion Notes

OUT WITH THE OLD...IN WITH THE NEW!

"Only love interests me, and I am only in contact with things I love."

-Marc Chagall, artist

CHAPTER FOURTEEN
Out With The Old. . .In With The New!

Do this with wild abandon! From your color list, we actually created a list of "Change." Don't forget that dark blue dress that represented the worst fight you and your lover had ever had. That fight had a life of its own, in living color...right there in your dark blue bedspread! The bedspread <u>must</u> go on the "change" list, and hopefully that blue dress is long gone.

It's amazing how things can hold negative energy. Use the previous chart and highlight the things you will keep in yellow highlighter. Use blue highlighter to mark the things you will be getting rid of, and use pink to highlight the things you will be keeping, but giving new life by painting, re-covering, or using in a new way.

Be honest. Don't leave something out because it cost too much money, or belonged to your grandmother. It doesn't necessarily mean you have to get rid of it completely. There may be a way to transform it into something workable. The bedspread could be covered with a duvet cover, or the furniture could be refinished and updated to suit your new color palette!

Are you on board the Passion Romance Express? The next several chapters will give you detailed information on how to arrive at your passion destination.

Your Passion Notes

CREATING YOUR BOUDOIR OF SEDUCTION

Women need a reason to have sex.
Men just need a place.
-Billy Crystal, actor and comedian

CHAPTER FIFTEEN
Creating Your Boudoir Of Seduction

At last...creating your own "boudoir of seduction!" Congratulations! You've put in a lot of hard work!

Where to begin? With the Passion by Design System™ you've educated yourself as to your likes, dislikes, wants, and needs. It's time to put your knowledge to work.

First and foremost, formulate your fantasy bedroom in your mind's eye. Think of anything and everything you want it to be. For ideas, in Section Two, you will find four steamy romantic fantasies with "Passion Blueprints™" for creating those fantasy bedrooms.

Now, let's assess your needs. Does part of your room need to be devoted to a computer desk? Think about ways to tuck it discreetly into your fantasy bedroom. A two or three-panel fabric or wooden screen can divide that part of your room nicely. What about floating your bed in the center of the room and putting the desk behind a faux wall you create by hanging yards of fabric or even plywood painted to complement the walls? It's amazing what a difference it can make. Storage can also be placed and concealed behind a bed.

Let's look at what you've got in your "Passion Bank Account". Start window-shopping. Get the price for paint, new fabric, and new bedding. Get rid of the idea that whatever you choose has to be expensive and have lasting appeal. It's simply not true. With careful shopping, you can find the furniture and fabrics of your <u>current</u> dreams, within a price that will make it possible for you to change when you are ready for something new. It just takes a little shopping and researching.

Invest your money in the things that really require good quality, like top of the line mattresses, 350 + thread count sheets, and good quality Egyptian cotton towels.

Buy 1/8 yard swatches of bedding fabric or a pillow to take with you to the paint store. Often, existing bedding can be enhanced with beautiful trims from fabric and upholstery shops. We'll give you more information about this later.

Consider fabrics and paint colors carefully and remember to select the fabric and carpet first because the colors are fixed. With paint, however, you can custom blend to complement any fabrics you choose.

Go into your bedroom and empty it. Ideally, it would be great to literally clear the room, as they do in the design shows. This gives you a completely fresh canvas to create your new masterpiece. If you can't completely clear it out, you can rid it of all the knick-knacks and clutter. You might bring some of these pieces back into your room, but for now—clear it out!

Clear it out! Doesn't it feel good! You're making room for your re-designed romantic life!

Your Passion Notes

THE ART OF DECORATIVE PAINTING

---❤---

"I do not literally paint that table, but the
emotion it produces upon me."

-Henri Matisse, artist

CHAPTER SIXTEEN
The Art Of Decorative Painting

"A home's interior is the natural projection of your soul."
-Coco Chanel

Painting a room is one of the least expensive and simplest ways to evoke a new feeling in your surroundings. It's also a change that you can make frequently because it is so easy to do.

Painting in an empty room is pleasurable; painting in a room full of furniture is a drag. You'll be surprised at how uplifted you'll feel to see the room freshly painted!

Passion Tip:
It is easier to blend the wall paint to go with your fabric, than to find fabric to match your wall paint.

Go to your nearest home improvement store and study paint chips. Take your Personal Passion Style™ Notebook along so you can pull paint chips from the display to compare them to colors in your design samples. Take the paint chips home and look at them in your room at different times during the day.

Color changes throughout the day. If you're having trouble choosing paint from the tiny swatch of color, invest in a quart (or smaller amount if your paint dealer allows) of the paint. Paint some onto a poster board and hang the board up in your room. Live with it for a day or two. If you fall in love with this color…go for it. Paint the whole room.

Remember the ceiling! Ceilings are no longer left white! Look at your white ceilings and notice that they <u>actually</u> register gray to the eye!

Paint your ceiling a color that complements, but doesn't overpower (lighter rather than darker). If the ceiling is high, you can be bold and go a little darker than if you have a lower ceiling. Ceilings in the great homes and buildings in Europe are always painted. Lest we not forget Michelangelo! You could even do a mural on the ceiling…and we're not talking about the "cutesy" skies with cloud puffs painted on blue. Sky ceilings well done can be wonderful.

Stenciling is also a nice touch *if it's done well.* Many people think of stenciling as primary color flowers, ivy, and curly cues. Not any more. There's a whole new world of stencils out there. Look to the Internet for some stencil companies, you'll be thrilled at the vast array of possibilities.

Choose something elegant that blends with the fantasy room you are going for. Perhaps bronze gilded fleur-de-lis (if you're doing our Paris bedroom in Section Two), in a few places to highlight. A little stenciling can be just the right touch…too much, and you've blown it. Try stenciling around a dresser mirror, or to accent the bathroom door. Use two or three colors. Layer on the first color, then go over it sporadically with another color, try a third color. That's just enough.

For many of Paula's higher end homes, she enlists renowned San Francisco artist, Lynne Rutter, to adorn walls and ceilings with magnificent murals. Lynne's work can be seen in some of the finest celebrity homes, churches, casinos and businesses across the United States.

Another way to enhance a room is by using decorative paint finishes. These may also be referred to as faux finishes (pronounced "foh"). Decorative painting is not a trend. This technique has been done for thousands of years. This painting technique is used to create illusion, mood, and beauty. It's the use of multiple colors and glazes washed over walls to create a desired affect. In today's homes, decorative painting is more desirable than ever before. With so many new homes being built, and older homes being remodeled, decorative art offers an opportunity to transform new homes into something magical… emotional…passionate…

In fact, decorative painting is now a staple in decorating. Choose to enlist the talent of a good decorative/faux artist in your area or learn how to do it yourself. We're not talking about simply sponge painting, for that is a misrepresentation of what the faux artist can achieve. We're talking about the use of brushes to rub and wash on layers of color, as well as other techniques in marbleizing, faux bois (wood graining, pronounced foh bwa), and Venetian plaster.

If you decide to do it yourself, be sure to practice on large sample boards. Bad faux can ruin a room instantly. Because wall space is a huge part of the room, nothing can create a more beautiful backdrop for your romantic room than faux done well.

For a truly professional "wall of art," employ a faux artist. Sean Decker of Decker Faux Artistry has had a hand in working in some of the most beautiful homes in Southern California. He states that faux painting can create the aura of romance, serenity, and bliss through an understanding and use of the "psychology of color." He reiterates what we covered in our chapter on color: certain hues evoke certain feelings. He helps his clients select color by presenting large sample boards they can live with for a few days. He was a partner in the team that transformed the celebrity home of Melissa Gilbert (of "Little House on the Prairie" fame).

From the outside, her home was a French chateau; on the inside was the challenge of 7500 square feet of white walls. Melissa stressed the importance of creating a master suite that offered a retreat of quiet serenity overlooking the mountains of Malibu.

Melissa had starred in a movie in Ireland and had the opportunity to actually film in some of the great castles of Ireland. Having grown up in a world of fantasy, she wanted to make her master suite reminiscent of a castle with walls, crumbling around the edges, breaking way to a view that may have ignited the great romance of Sir Lancelot and Lady Guinevere.

Sean Decker, along with a mural artist, painted walls with texture and light, creating the appearance of stone-blocked wall and, exposed bricks. He fauxaged the furniture to give a feeling of history. The faux stone-blocked walls broke away to a serene mural evocative of the Irish countryside. The ceiling was painted to give the illusion of exposed sky, rich with blue, lavender, and peach (no white puffy clouds!). The exposed wooden beams were draped with twisted vines and ivy. It was the ultimate romantic setting for Melissa and her handsome husband, actor Bruce Boxleitner.

Painting is hard work. If you're up for it, great! If not, ask your paint store for a recommendation of a painter that can come into your home and paint your dream bedroom for you. Ask the painter for client references, especially when it comes to faux. Figure the cost into your budget. You'll see the end result will be well worth it!

Your Passion Notes

DRESSING YOUR BEDROOM FOR PASSION!

"Where love is, no room is too small."

-Talmud

CHAPTER SEVENTEEN
Dressing Your Bedroom For Passion!

Melissa Gilbert is more than a talented actress. She has a wonderful decorating vision, and chose fabrics of silk velvets, brocades, and rich trims for her magical room. When asked about her personal decorating tip, she stressed the importance of change.

"I change the bedding, the fabrics, the throws, even the pillows on the chaise as often as the seasons. I go for lighter colors and fabrics in the spring and summer, and heavier, cozier fabrics with rich colors in the winter and fall."
-Melissa Gilbert, actress

Action Steps: Begin by bringing in one piece of furniture at a time. See it with a new eye. Could the bed possibly be angled against the corner of the room? Would it look better to have the sitting area by the window? Buy the plastic disks called "Furniture Movers" that make it easy to push furniture around.

Consider buying high thread count sheets. Good quality sheets withstand years of washing and feel soft and silky to the touch. Incorporate colors that flatter, colors that awaken passion, and colors that soothe after a long day. Have mounds of down pillows available for cushioning, caressing, propping, squish-ing...and sleeping.

Buy sheets that complement your skin tone. Think about it…would you wear a shade of green if it made your skin look green? No! Never! Remember that, your beautiful naked body will be sprawled across the bed on top of whatever shade of sheets you choose. Make sure it brings out the best in your skin tone.

The same goes with bath towels and your bathrobe. Are they colors that complement your bare skin and face (sans make-up)? Towels are an important bath accessory that can lend a blast of color to your skin and your bathroom. Don't hide them in cupboards. Buy extras to roll up in a basket beside your bath.

One inexpensive way to dress your bed might be the purchase of a simple but elegant duvet cover or bedspread, and two pillow shams in a luxurious solid color that suits the style and theme of your fantasy bedroom.

Now, go to the fabric store with one of the pillows. You're going to coordinate another fabric and trims to make your new bedspread look fabulous. It's important to choose a fabric at the upholstery or fabric store that is so beautiful it takes your breath away. You're only going to need 3 to 4 yards, so don't be scared off by what seems to be a high price tag. Buy an inexpensive yard of coordinating fabric for the back of the pillows (no one ever sees it, and it saves money). Select coordinating decorative bouillon, fringe, or cord. Either sewing or the all-purpose glue gun will attach these. Don't forget to buy pillow forms to stuff your pillows.

Here's the list for your throw and pillows:
- 2-3 yards fabric (allow more if you're making your pillows)
- Decorative bouillon, ribbons, fringe or cording
- Pillow forms
- Coordinating inexpensive fabric for backing your pillows
- Thread
- Glue gun and glue sticks
- Colorful pillows if you are not going to make your own

Continue reading to get the full picture of what you'll be doing. Also, you can ask the person helping you at the fabric store to guide you with the correct yardage of everything. They are typically very good at helping you if you describe what you are creating.

Cut a two and a half yard section of your drop dead gorgeous fabric and sew the edges to make a throw. Fold it in half lengthwise and sew or glue gun the edges closes. This will be draped across the end of your bed. Trim it with bouillon or fabric cord. If you're using a glue gun for the trim, be careful...it gets very hot!

Drape the throw across the bottom of the bed, across the duvet. Make a few pillows (backed with the inexpensive fabric) that coordinate with the throw. If you don't know how to sew pillows, just cut two rectangles from the breathtaking fabric and the inexpensive fabric you will be backing it with. Sew together on three edges. Stuff with a pillow form, then tie as though you are tying a gift bag with a section of cording or ribbon.

The alternative to making a pillow is to purchase a simple pillow in a color that complements your new duvet or bedspread. Cut wide bands (12 inches or more) of the beautiful fabric to fit completely around your pillow. Glue gun a hem on all edges, then sew or glue the band in a circle. Put the band of fabric around the pillow (in a complementary fabric). Glue gun the band closed. Slip the band around the pillow and attach with a small stitch, or if you must...a small hidden safety pin. It can be easily slipped off when it's time for a change!

The beauty of this investment is you can change the look of your room, without having to make a heavy investment in an all-new duvet or bedspread and pillow shams. You can simply make a new throw and a few new pillows. Voila! The bedding looks completely new!

Nightstands are a master suite staple. Choose the height so it is convenient to reach, and make sure it has a deep enough drawer...and possibly a lock... for your naughty toys and pleasure tools.

Set the top of it with lamps for reading that also have dimmer switches for setting the mood. A good lamp store can often replace the existing switch with a dimmer for a nominal charge.

Keep a crystal carafe or a hand painted ceramic water pitcher with goblets on a tray on top of your nightstand. After a night of passion, one often wakes up with a ravaging thirst that needs quenching. Also, keep a dish of mints on each side of the bed for freshening your breath for that first-thing in the morning romp! Fresh flowers also bring color and life into your bedroom.

Designate a place in your suite as your sanctuary…a place where you can read, write in your journal, or close your eyes to refresh yourself. Keep your CD player close by to enhance your delicious respite with music.

Passion Tip
Avoid cluttering your boudoir: when you add a purchase, give something away. Someone else will really appreciate your gift. The other option (if you just can't part with it) is to put it into storage to give you time to fall in love with it again. Clutter is stressful. Keep clearing.

Action Steps: Dress the stage! Go around your home and find accessories for your new room. Go into cupboards, drawers, and the attic…anywhere you might have a treasure that could be a part of your new look. A silver tea service, already tarnished and aged would look great sitting on the upholstered ottoman in front of your chair. Hang a sexy negligee on a fabric-padded hanger on the closet door. Decorate with a long strand of pearls and a silk rose. Find antique plates for candles and long stemmed wineglasses for floating votive candles.

Music is an important tool for setting the stage and…sorry, Guys…there's nothing beautiful about an audio system. You could hide the speakers with plants, or tuck them discreetly behind furniture.

Here's something to consider about exercise equipment. Dreams of physical transformation accompany the purchase of that brand new, expensive piece of exercise equipment. Perhaps it's a stationary bicycle, a treadmill, a stair stepper…whatever. It doesn't belong in the bedroom!

More than likely it is now a hanger for used clothing, belts or ties. It's also a constant reminder of what you are <u>not</u> doing! Move it elsewhere, the garage, the den, the spare bedroom! Join a gym or create a mini gym in another room or garage that inspires you to work out. Paint it in bold colors.

Hang pictures that motivate you…the beaches of Hawaii where you'll want to sport your new body in a stunning bathing suit. If you are sharing the room as part of something else, use a three-piece screen to block it off. Make it your private gym where the body of your dreams is just a commitment away! Good luck!

Your Passion Notes

WINDOWS TO LOVE

———————————————♥———————————————
"You see things; and you say 'Why?' But I dream things that never were; and I say 'Why not?"
                    -George Bernard Shaw. playwright
_____

CHAPTER EIGHTEEN
Windows To Love

Windows connect us to the great outdoors. Window treatments i.e. curtains, and draperies and window coverings are the final statement of your "romance suite." Take the opportunity to reveal your room's personality with sweeps of color that boldly swathe and frame your outside <u>and</u> inside world. A nice mix of treatments can offer the most versatility. Instead of heavy drapes, consider sheer panels or matchstick bamboo shades that can allow light in a dark room during the day. They filter sunlight, provide some privacy, and soften the view outside.

Watch out, though! If you notice an audience gathering outside every night, it's because sheer panels and shades become transparent at night if the inside lights are on! Try layering heavier panels over the sheers, you will have more privacy for night...and lovemaking.

If you use sheer panels and you like to leave the window open, be careful of nearby candles! Another safe alternative: battery operated candles.

Even if you don't need window treatments for privacy, we recommend you use them to enhance and finish the decor of the room. It's what a frame does for a painting. It gives it that finishing touch.

Window treatments are a finishing statement to your fantasy bedroom. They are like a touch of lipstick to complete your look.

You can make inexpensive rods and brackets look elegant by spray-painting them with hammered gold, bronze, black, or any color you choose. Choose coordinating tassels to tie draperies back. They can cost a lot, or a little, depending on where you buy them.

One client found some plain and simple silk drapes at a discount store for a nominal cost. She trimmed the hem with some bouillon fringe and her glue gun. They were amazing and looked like they had cost a fortune!

You, too, can achieve a high-end decorator look by layering multiple fabrics in the window treatments with contrasting fabrics. Beads, bouillon trims, crystals, braids, buttons-all can be added on as trims to make your fabrics look richer.

Let your imagination be wrapped in layers of fantasy…and fabrics.

Your Passion Notes

LIGHTING IS A GIRL'S BEST FRIEND

"The difference between pornography and erotica is lighting."

-Gloria Leonard

CHAPTER NINETEEN
Lighting Is A Girl's Best Friend

Ask any actress on a movie set and she will tell you that the cinematographer is the key to looking like a star! The cinematographer spends hours with his crew, designing optimum lighting, using filters, back lights, overhead lights; the list goes on.

There was a secret technique used many years ago of smearing Vaseline over the lens of the camera to soften the lines of aging actresses. Lighting is the magic to make you appear softer, more sensuous, more dreamy. Lighting our bedrooms romantically casts the light of love in our fantasy bedrooms! There are ways to create that soft illusory mood, as though you are making love in soft focus.

The Passion Pink Light Bulb Trick
Paula recommends buying soft pink light bulbs for bedside lamps. Try holding your hand under the light of a regular light bulb. Now change the bulb and look at the difference. Your skin is suddenly softer, suppler, and more touchable! It's the mood lighting of love.

An additional secret of the stars is lining your bedroom lampshades with pink silk. Be careful to keep the wattage on the light bulbs low to prevent the silk from scorching. This technique is guaranteed to amp up his wattage!

There are three important things to keep in mind when choosing lighting for your romantic bedroom:

Ambient light: This type of lighting is general lighting in the room that keeps you from running into things! Typically, in American homes, a single fixture placed smack dab in the center of the room, is the first light to go on. It is usually not the most flattering of lights, and is one that you most likely do not want glaring down on your lovemaking...especially without a dimmer.

Task Lighting: This lighting is designed so that you can see to do a specific task. This might be reading a book, putting on make-up, or playing our new Passion By Design Board Game™ with your lover. Lamps that can adjust up and down or swivel tend to be more versatile. People have different needs in reading lights. A good strong halogen lamp on a dimmer offers versatility.

Accent or Decorative Lighting: This lighting is used to highlight art, sculpture, plants, or any area of the room to which you'd like to draw the attention. The secret here is contrast. You want to have a focused light emphasizing special objects to make them visually "pop." Accent lighting is most effectively created with low voltage halogen lights. Halogen lighting gives wonderful clear, white light that we often see in restaurants. It makes crystal and silver sparkle! Spotlights offer directed pinpointed light to accent a specific object. The selection of a flood bulb gives a softer, more diffused, decorative light.

Fortunately, halogen light bulbs are now available in a size that screws directly into your regular lighting socket. Be careful of two things:

1) Halogen bulbs can get extremely hot. Don't ever touch a bulb that is on. Let them cool quite awhile before changing them or touching them.

2) Do not ever touch the tiny halogen bulbs that go into torchères with your bare fingers, as the oil from your hands will make them burn hotter and cause them to burn out much sooner. Use gloves, hold with a tissue, or wipe them off thoroughly if you happen to touch them. The industry is taking measures to eliminate this step, but for now, better just be safe and do it.

Do you purchase lighting or remodel what you have? Assess the existing lighting and decide if it suits the style of your fantasy room. You can change the look of existing lamps and lighting by changing lampshades, or trimming them with beads, crystals, or whatever your heart's desire. Hand painting or stenciling a lampshade is also a possibility.

If your overhead light is one of those generic fixtures installed by the builder, replace it, or try toning down the look by aging it with a burnt umber glaze (found with decorative painting supplies).

Chandeliers can be an amazing look for a bedroom! Add crystals wherever you can, for they cast enchanting light that dances around the room.

Passion Tip
Dimmer switches are a <u>must</u> for any overhead lighting. In fact every light in your home should be on a dimmer. Dimmers offer great versatility and are relatively simple to install.

We all want to be seen in the best possible light...especially when our clothes are off!

Candlelight is the most sensual light you can choose. It combines flame and heat and passion. Try to choose your scented candles carefully. Select one or two good quality scented candles and the rest unscented.

For safety in the bedroom, put the candle on a plate or shallow bowl filled with water. In a moment of passion, a candle could be knocked over! Always use caution when using candles.

Place candles in shallow bowls or plates with water. When the candle burns all the way down, it should extinguish itself.

Your Passion Notes

A WORD ABOUT WORDS

♥

Let's turn our attention from the bedroom blueprint, back to the relationship blueprint. It all works together to create your life of passion!

CHAPTER TWENTY
A Word About Words

Words are used to transfer information from one person to another. Think of your mind as a fully functional computer. What you see, hear, taste smell, and touch gets recorded on our brain's hard drive. The words you speak and the words you hear are filed and can be accessed over and over again.

Last night's words of love are on the "Love File." This morning's disagreement over the burnt toast is in the "Bump in the Relationship" file. For some odd reason, our brains make it easier to access the negative words and thoughts than the positive ones.

Simple adjustments in the way you phrase things can turn a negative into a positive. One little trick is to change the word "but" to "and" when you respond.

Words are difficult to erase once they are spoken. For example if you say: "Honey, I understand why you think the bedroom walls should be purple, *but* I wanted lighter colors." This sends the message to your mate that his idea was bad! Choose your words with a positive flair. Try this little change: "Honey, I understand why you think the bedroom walls should be purple, it's your favorite color, *and* we could also incorporate some lighter colors, maybe some shades of lavender and pinks. Let's see what we can come up with."

Do you see how much more pleasant the second way sounded? It enlisted his help rather than alienate his idea as a horrible one. He feels validated! Still worried about that purple?

More than likely, it was a passing thought with him; and because you didn't fight him on it, he didn't draw a line in the sand. You'll be able to negotiate the color rather than have to go into battle for it.

Words set the stage for feelings. Think about how you refer to your mate. If you call him "Daddy" in front of the children, he sees you as "Mommy." Stop! Isn't that what the children call him? You're not one of his children, and you are on a quest to become a more desirable sexual woman.

You might consider calling him, "Darling" or "Sweetheart" because that creates a picture in his mind of his lover calling his name…not his "Mommy." This also sets a positive role model for your children when they grow up and have love relationships of their own.

♥

Our words and perceptions are a self-fulfilling prophecy. Change your words and perceptions…and you change your life.

The same situation, event, or picture evokes totally different images and reactions to each of us. The powerful point of this information is that we can change our perceptions by changing the story we tell ourselves about ourselves or a particular person, place, situation, or thing.

Notice the words you use in describing your relationship and how they paint the pictures of your reality. You will begin to see your vocabulary's strengths and weaknesses.

Scolding is the fastest way to make that big brawny man of yours revert back to the little boy…in more ways than one! We strongly recommend that you avoid doing it! Ever!

Using encouragement is a better tactic than admonishing. For instance, if you feel your mate is less than available for making love, instead of saying "You never make time for sex anymore!" Try instead: *"I have been thinking about making love to you all day. I've got something special in mind…who knows? Maybe my fantasies are your fantasies. How about tonight?"*

Turn your thoughts into your spoken words and you have a remarkable tool for shaping your future. Anthony Robbins, a world-renowned motivational speaker and author, emphasizes the importance of making detailed lists of the kind of future you want. He stresses that putting your dreams in writing sets your future in motion. Taking the time to define, *in words*, empowers you to get what you want in life...and the love you desire!

Tell him:
"I have been thinking about making love to you all day. I've got something special in mind...who knows; maybe my fantasies are *your* fantasies.
How about tonight..."

TERMS OF ENDEARMENT

Write a list of all the names you call your husband, and how you refer to him:

1) When speaking with him personally. (Example: "Honey," "Sweetie,")

2) When speaking to him around the children. (Example: "Daddy")

3) When referring to him with others. (Example: "The man in my life," or "my husband")

4) What you call him when you're angry or irritated. (Example: "Yes, dear")

5) What you call him while making love. (Example: "Baby")

6) Write the names that your lover uses for <u>you.</u>

7) Write the terms of endearment you would like your partner to use when referring to you.

And finally…analyze this list and start implementing words that are more reflective of a couple still madly in love, and passionately adored.

"No man is exempt from saying silly things; the mischief is to say them deliberately."
-Michel Yequem de Montaigne

Your Passion Notes

CHANGES AND CHOICES

"All mankind's inner feelings eventually manifest themselves as an outer reality."

-Stuart Wilde, Author

CHAPTER TWENTY-ONE
Changes And Choices

Most of us deal with change the way we dealt with being born. We were pulled along, kicking and screaming. And guess what? We were born anyway, whether we liked it or not.

Since change is inevitable, our philosophy is to *embrace* it, rather than resist it.

"What you resist, persists."
-Carl Jung

When we decide to embrace change, and reshape our attitude that change is desirable, then change becomes our strongest ally and friend, rather than something to be fought or feared.

When we operate from a position of choice and power, rather than the position of victim, we command, conquer, and regain our power over the inevitable. Imagine how much more fun you will have when you become the change agent, in control of, in fact, the motivating factor for change.

It is an immutable facet of the feminine nature to be mutable, changeable, mercurial, capricious, and unpredictable. Cultivate the delight that your lover will have when he realizes that the changes you make are with a constant intention to pleasure *him*.

- Choice: Gliding on a bit of lipstick in the morning.
- Choice: Spraying yourself lightly with a bath splash upon rising.
- Choice: Wearing a robe that flatters your skin tone, especially when you are not wearing make-up.

All of these choices are as easy to make as preparing your morning coffee, and yet, these choices send an important message to your lover.

The messages are subtle, often subliminal, but they tell your mate that you care about yourself and the reflection you see in his eyes! When he sees you with a hint of color on your lips in the morning, he may not consciously register that you have applied make-up. All he registers is that your face is aglow, and your lips look desirable and kissable.

Ladies, it's a known fact that our skin loses underlying color, and dare we say it…fades as we age. Sad, but true. What about the countless songs written about ruby colored lips dazzling your man? Keep the legend going strong by taking a moment to wash those lips in color with a little lip stain or lipstick… blot…then give your man a kiss to launch his morning into high gear.

Here's a designer makeup tip: when you apply your blush in the morning, re-load the brush so the next morning you can simply brush it lightly across your cheeks and voila, instantly create a more youthful look. If you put your makeup brushes in a beautiful standup crystal glass or container, they will be readily accessible and kept in good condition.

Remember, we are surrounding our world with colors that flatter. The color you select for your bathrobe is essential. Its color should flatter your skin sans make-up. Colors that enhance your face without make-up might be peach, pink, apricot, and turquoise; and for woman of color, try red, mocha, creams, or ivories. If your robe is white, make sure it's a shade of white that flatters your skin tone.

Passion Tip
That which we use daily should be exquisite.
Use your finest crystal, your beautiful linens,
and luxurious bath products every day!

Buy beautiful robes, nightgowns, rich soaps, hand towels; even your hair-brush and toothbrush should be selected in beautiful styles and colors. You're worth it!

Your Passion Notes

MEN AND THE ART OF CHANGE

"Do all things with love."

-Og Mandino

CHAPTER TWENTY-TWO
Men And The Art Of Change

Women enjoy changing their environment to enhance beauty and purpose, while men seem to focus first and foremost on comfort. When coming to design changes, Paula says the phrase she hears most often from men is, "It's fine, why do you want to change it?" Understanding this seemingly male trait (sorry for the generalization!) is absolutely necessary in considering how you go about making the changes in your relationship <u>and</u> your bedroom.

A friend of ours was set on changing her kitchen. She wanted to use the colors of Tuscany. She was about to spend thousands of dollars when her husband yelled "Time out on the play!" He asked her why she needed to redo the kitchen when it worked fine the way it was, and besides he'd be just as happy if everything were painted black...his favorite color. Obviously this man was not the kind of husband who drew great satisfaction in finding just the right hue of Tuscany gold at the home improvement store that afternoon!

Now our friend hated black. Uh oh, we have the foundation for a huge disagreement here! But guess what! Our friend was brilliant... "Honey," she said, "You just gave me a great idea! I think we should paint the center island cabinetry in black!"

And they did! They incorporated a distressed black finish on the island cabinets, and it was just the right touch to spark her Tuscany kitchen, <u>and</u> her relationship.

Imagine how validated **he** felt when they unveiled their kitchen at a dinner party several weeks later and **she** proudly acknowledged, *"It was my husband who had the great idea for the color of the center island."*

"A man thinks "function," a woman thinks "esthetics."

He's got an old leather chair that is **his** chair and he loves it. He's mystified when she wants to replace it. "It's comfortable," he says.

"It looks terrible and I'm embarrassed when my friends and family see it, everything else is so beautiful," she retorts. They are at an impasse. Passion by Design to the rescue!

She needs to feel proud of her home, and her home is a reflection and an artistic expression of who she is. *He* needs to feel comfortable and his things need to feel familiar.

Here are three possible options for our passion couple to get what they both want:

- Choice 1: She shops for the newer, more comfortable version of the chair without the saggy seat cushions and broken springs. She has him try it before purchasing!
- Choice 2: She creates a beautiful slipcover from fabric, which coordinates with the rest of the room, and buys him a new, fancier remote control to slip in a pocket she's provided on the side.
- Choice 3: She takes his chair, with his permission, to a professional upholsterer who recovers it and suggests adding nail head accents. Guess what...he loves it!

With all of these choices, she has been the instrument of increasing his comfort and pleasure level. Imagine how inspired and motivated he'll be to increase her pleasure!

Your Passion Notes

THE TIRED BEDROOM SYNDROME

"If love is blind, why is lingerie so popular?"

- Unknown

CHAPTER TWENTY-THREE
The Tired Bedroom Syndrome

Do you ever have days where you can find nothing to wear in your closet (that happens to be jammed with clothes), because there is *not one* single item of clothing that feels like who you are today? We call it being in "clothing crisis." It's a symptom of the virus known as the "Tired Closet Syndrome."

Fret not, it happens to the best of us. No matter how many clothes we have, it can come over us in the blink of an eye, ravage our self-esteem, and wreak havoc with our well-being.

Here's how it starts. You have an event to attend. You want to look your best because there are going to be women at this event who work with your husband. Your husband is loyal and true, but every time you see these women, they speak of how wonderful your husband is…how funny, how talented, how they love, love, love working with him, etc.

It's wonderful to hear, but it almost feels like you don't know this man they speak of. It's a world outside of your relationship. You feel odd, a little unsettled, and even wonder if any of these women might be attracted to your man.

Of course they are! But he loves **you**! Now, faced with having to be present at another co-worker love fest, you have to find just the right outfit to make you look like the knockout you are, and know that your man is proud to have you on his arm.

Oh no! You look through your closet, and you look again, and again. You may have looked at the clothes in your closet a hundred times and know exactly what you have, but tonight, nothing seems right. You don't have time to shop for anything new. How about your long black dress?

No…everyone will be wearing black, and you want to shine. You love the persimmon colored cashmere sweater because it makes your skin look so creamy, but the winter white wool skirt you pair it with, isn't quite dressy enough. How about wearing the royal blue damask skirt? The white beaded tank is what you always wear with it, but this event is outdoors. Now what?

Clothing flies with wild abandon until you've tried on virtually everything in your closet. Nothing seems to work.

Alas!

Suddenly your eyes catch sight of the persimmon colored cashmere sweater tossed haphazardly on top of the royal blue damask skirt. Paired together, persimmon and royal blue…the colors knock you out! Why hadn't you ever seen this combination before? You put it on, and your husband looks at you with awe. He sees it… the confidence you exude when the outfit is "right." It is your night to shine. You are now transformed and ready to re-introduce yourself to the man you love.

Well girls, the "tired closet syndrome" comes from the **same** virus as the "tired bedroom syndrome." Your bedroom is so tired, it suddenly becomes the place where sleep is the only thing you think about because you are bored to death with the same colors, furniture, and accessories.

You find it difficult to imagine your bed being placed anywhere but between the two windows on the eastern wall. You have the same color scheme going on because you've painted the walls light blue, and everything matches the light blue.

Voila! You have the "tired bedroom syndrome" which wreaks havoc on your sex life, and your relationship! The *Passion By Design System* offers you numerous ways to re-think the state of your bedroom. We suggest you go for broke!

Transformations can happen purposefully or accidentally (like our persimmon sweater and royal blue skirt). Do you think the clothing actually changes who you are? No. But it does give your attitude an adjustment. Perhaps we should clothe ourselves with affirmations that make us feel sexual, gorgeous, confident, fun, frisky, adventurous, the list goes on.

Actresses do it every time they call "action!" Do you think they feel sexy and desirable all the time? Absolutely not! When cameras roll, they clothe themselves in ATTITUDE!

For attitude inspiration, download our free Passion Attitude Cards.™ from our website at **www.PassionByDesign.com**.

Download these cards onto heavy paper, cut them up, and place them in a beautiful box by your bed. Use them to tune up that attitude *and* your sex life!

Start every day by pulling out one of these cards and repeat the affirmation to yourself over and over again in front of a mirror. Then, repeat again while you are driving to work, and periodically throughout the day. If they include assignments, *do them*. The assignments are the tools to affirm your new romantic life. You'll find them fun and rewarding!

Your Passion Notes

MASTERING THE ART OF FLIRTING

♥

"Sex appeal is something that you feel deep down inside. It's suggested rather than shown. I'll admit that I'm not as well-stacked as Sophia Loren or Gina Lollabrigida, but there is more to sex appeal than just measurements."

-Audrey Hepburn, actress

CHAPTER TWENTY-FOUR
Mastering The Art Of Flirting

It is an enviable woman who has mastered the art of flirting. What feels more wonderful than to be flirted with, paid attention to, flattered, and admired. Whether a woman is nineteen or ninety, it is her God given right to flirt and be flirted with. When we fully explore the wellspring of flirting, life becomes richer, fuller, and doggonnit!... more fun!

Listen to one of our own stories...

Sandy was unexpectedly divorced after 25 years of marriage. It was a surprise to all who knew her, but Sandy was determined to enrich her life with new opportunities. She had heard that being divorced and in your forties is a chance to be an adolescent all over again. Those years can be the teenage years of the rest of your life! She took a year to gather her life together, then set out on a journey to rediscover dating.

Sandy went to parties, gallery openings, concerts...all of the right places to meet new people. She wasn't interested in getting right into another relationship, just casual dating. She missed the friendship she had had with her husband, and looked forward to finding male friendship with others. Weeks went by... nothing. Months went by...nothing. She finally asked her therapist for some suggestions. "Sandy," she stated, "Your red stoplight has been turned on for twenty five years, it's time to turn the green light back on!"

She was right! Many of us who have been in long-term relationships have forgotten what it's like to flirt. As soon as we got married, we subconsciously turned on the red stoplight. Somehow, we thought that flirting was reserved for the single woman. Not true! Flirting can be perfectly harmless, but oh so good for the self-esteem. We're suggesting you turn the green light back on and start flirting!

What is the pheromone that attracts the opposite sex? A friend of ours recounts the story of Olivia, a woman well in her 70's. When at social gatherings, men seemed to flock around Olivia as men did around Scarlett O'Hara in "Gone With the Wind." Whether they were in their 30's, 50's, or 90's, Olivia always had their attention. Our friend inquired of one of the gentlemen who knew her, "What is it about Olivia that men love?" The young man replied, "Ah...Olivia. Because when you talk to her, she makes you feel like you are the only man alive."

Master flirting is like a magician's sleight of hand. It is imperceptible to others, but undeniable to those involved. It is eye contact held just a second longer...a smile which stays on the lips, just a second longer...a knowing touch that lingers, just a second longer.

Experiment
The next time you are with him, think about making love... or lust! Look into his eyes and think of your bodies together. Transfer the pleasure to his eyes. We guarantee this will ignite his desire. It's the power of the mind!

There is tremendous power in a look or a brief gaze. A seemingly artless graze of a hand on his shoulder, or a glint of some secret amusement, something that only you know, but that he is dying to learn, ...these are the foundations of mastering the art of flirting. All that's needed is a little practice!

Your Passion Notes

BANKING ON PASSION

♥
"Love has nothing to do with what you are expecting to get—only with what you are expecting to give—which is everything."
-Katherine Hepburn, actress

CHAPTER TWENTY-FIVE
Banking On Passion

Money can have either positive or negative connotations in our daily lives. Paying for a vacation... your tax bill...negative. It's important that the renovation of your passionate life be surrounded with pleasant and joyful feelings. We don't want you sitting in your new boudoir, worrying about the credit card bill that is due to pay for your beautiful new love retreat.

You're writing the check for Passion. Make it happen and spare no expense. You and your lover are worth it.

Start your planning by having a discussion with your lover over a good glass of red wine and a delicious tray of fresh cheese with soft music and the potential for an evening of making love. Remember, it's all about setting the stage!

Discuss your budget for the room <u>only</u>. Don't fall into a talk about your national debt, or how you're going to pay for your children to go to college. Start by discussing the bedroom of your fantasies and approximating what you think each change will roughly cost. Changes can be made in increments. Discussing the room by breaking down the costs makes it feel more doable.

Open a separate bank account for your bedroom. Nickname it "The Passion Account." Write checks from it as you need it, and only for purchases for your bedroom! You can start by putting an amount you feel comfortable with into the account. Add to it, a little at a time, much like a Christmas fund. We encourage you to only make the changes, as you feel comfortable in your financial situation. Credit cards are a no, no. Too much negative energy once the bills roll in. We know you're anxious, but you can always start with paint, which makes a huge change for very little money.

There's an advantage to bringing your ideas and designs to slow fruition. The passion concept of design is one that is meant to be a pathway to the ultimate goal…a rewarding and fulfilling romantic life set in serene and beautiful surroundings where the soul can never go dormant. The interior design shows on television often tout the instant gratification factor. Don't fall into this trap. Enjoy the discovery and creative process. Coax it, nurture it, savor it, for you'll appreciate it more with each and every change you make, and the value it has in the room. *And* of course, your love life.

Your Passion Notes

TIME TO LOVE

"Immature love says;
"I love you because I need you." Mature love says:
"I need you because I love you."

-Erich Fromm

CHAPTER TWENTY-SIX
Time To Love

One of the most important aspects of creating your place of love is the time you spend together. The creative process is stimulating to all the senses! When the two of you are sharing ideas, it connects you on a deeper spiritual level that is an aphrodisiac in itself! You are *both* participants in your love relationship... therefore; you should include each other in design of your boudoir!

If one partner makes all the decisions, the purchases, and the changes, the other may feel like an onlooker instead of a participant. Your partner might even be a little resentful with the output of money that was not made by mutual agreement. How can you get a reluctant participant to get involved?

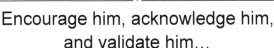

Encourage him, acknowledge him, and validate him... the rewards will be yours.

Really listen to the ideas he or she may have. Don't throw the ideas away because you had something different in mind. A conversation might go like this:

He says, "Honey, I really liked the bright orange bedspread we saw in Mexico" (you're thinking an orange bedspread wouldn't go at all with the soft peach walls you had in mind). Instead of putting his idea down and replying "that's a terrible idea...it doesn't go with peach at all," try something like this: "I like that idea! Orange really is a bold, passionate color, we could incorporate it into our room with points of color, like in paintings, or candles, or flowers!"

Amazing! You have validated his idea, made him feel good about himself, and he loves you more because he feels good in your presence.

And…don't worry about that orange in your peach room. Take a lesson from nature…dots of color can be blended if they are colors of nature. For instance, a flowerbed of purples and deep crimson can be brought to life with a few bedding plants in yellow and orange.

Is your partner not much of a shopper? Bring samples of fabrics and paints home. Over a lingering cup of coffee and croissants in bed on a Sunday morning, bring out the swatches and pictures of things you would like to do (with promises of the things you would like to do to him!). Ask him how he thinks certain colors look against your skin…how certain fabrics feel against his body, and yours.

Make shopping trips an adventure. Make it a fun day by incorporating shopping with the reward of a blissful lunch and wine tasting at your favorite winery. Men generally are not long distance power shoppers. Remember, your room will develop over time. Shop just a little at a time. It will give you the best excuse to plan many wonderful days with your spouse. It also gives you a memory album full of times you spent together, those memories being triggered in your very own room. "Sweetheart, remember when we bought our candle sconces? I really enjoyed that day with you."

Remember…your bedroom should be a work in progress that is always dynamic and ever changing, like your love.

When your eyes and your senses become immune to the beauty of the room you are creating, it's time to make changes. Perhaps it just needs to be refreshed by moving furniture or re-arranging accessories. (Remember: he never gets tired of hearing you compliment him on his ideas <u>and</u> his brawn!). You could invite your partner to spend another "acquisition" afternoon with you followed by a couple's massage at your day spa. Just as your love evolves, your bedroom should be constantly evolving and changing.

Now comes the fun…let your creativity begin!

Your Passion Notes

THE SENSES & THEIR ROLE IN
ROMANTIC AMBIANCE

"The best kind of love is the kind that awakens the soul, makes us reach for more, plants a fire in our hearts, and brings peace to our minds."

-"The Notebook" movie

CHAPTER TWENTY-SEVEN
The Senses & Their Role In Romantic Ambiance

Remember the last time you bought a piece of furniture, painted, or decorated a room in your home? It had raised the level of your brain activity because it was new, fresh, and invigorating. Every time you entered the room, your eyes were drawn to it and your network of cells felt a pleasing sensation. After awhile, your brain became used to it and it didn't quite have the emotional impact it once had when it was new.

The same can be said for scents. Using the same signature perfume every day becomes routine and expected. When your lover kisses you on the nape of the neck it's a familiar smell. What happens if you interrupt the brain pattern with something new? It raises the brain's level of interest!

Stimulating the RAS (or Reticular Activating System) alerts the brain to notice new stimuli. The Passion by Design System works the RAS by continually stimulating the brain with new sights, smells, sounds, tastes, and touches.

We've chosen to add a sixth sense, the *passion sense*. . .the sense of romance! In the next section of the book, you will be guided through a romantic fantasy, followed by the process of creating a new bedroom that stimulates the six (yes 6!) senses.

Once you understand the importance of stimulating the senses in sustaining a deep, passionate, sensual, loving relationship, you will always want to include it in your life.

Your Passion Notes

PART TWO

PASSION BY DESIGN: THE FANTASIES
COME TO LIFE!

TROPICAL ISLAND RETREAT

"...someday my wish is for him to hold me in his arms, in a sea of deep blue, together at last, together as two."

-"Can't Buy Me Love," movie

CHAPTER TWENTY-EIGHT
Tropical Island Retreat

You walk the deserted beach of a lush tropical island, alone, Mai Tai in hand. The white sandy beach contrasts brilliantly with the clear turquoise and the ultramarine blue of the ocean. Your skin glistens in the heat of the late afternoon setting sun.

You notice a couple down the shore, ducking behind a mound of sand surrounded by low palms and colorful orchids that shimmer from the spray of the last wave. They hold each other in an intimate embrace.

Embarrassed, you turn to walk in the other direction. Through the sounds of the waves crashing on the shore, your own breath moves to the rhythm. Your hand touches your stomach. It feels lean. You feel good, even sexy; since your body had really responded to the health and wellness program you've been following the last several months. You feel energy you've not felt in a long time, even a sense of emotional lifting. It was satisfying to find your body fit beautifully in the revealing bathing suit you are wearing.

You needed this vacation to re-connect with yourself and with your lover. You have both been working long, hard hours. You look at this vacation as the beginning of your new passionate life.

Your feet sink into the wet sand and you notice a perfectly formed shell glistening in the lapping wave at your feet. You reach to pick it up, and it's pulled away from you by the tide. You chase after it and finally pluck it from the water several feet down shore. As you marvel at its beauty, you hear a moan. You turn your head and see the beautiful couple not far from you, embracing, excited, and unaware of your presence.

You quickly duck behind a nearby palm tree. You watch as this perfectly sculpted man pulls his incredibly exotic looking woman into him. He reaches lovingly, into the top of her bikini, caressing her breast. You feel guilty excitement, an unexpected voyeur. Your stomach tightens with desire.

In the distance you hear the ritual sound of the conch shell, announcing the setting of the sun…you feel sensual excitement, but you are alone. Your lover was expected last night, but his meeting schedule got changed and he had to take his chances on getting a plane reservation. It was supposed to be your first vacation together in forever. It's been a long time since you've felt a desire for romance. Life had been busy and intrusive. It was time to find each other again. However, his job and the airlines weren't cooperating.

You discreetly look at the sensuous couple in the distance. Her back is pressed against an island palm. They are enraptured with each other's bodies. He's kissing her neck urgently, moving down to her heaving breasts. Sighing, the woman wraps one leg around him, pulling his groin to hers.

You quiver; wishing the man you loved was beside you. You take a sip of your Mai Tai. The setting sun is blinding, and you lift your hand to shield your eyes. There's a tall figure walking toward you. You're embarrassed; you were caught watching the heated couple. You turn, walking away.

You sense a presence drawing near and quicken your pace. Startled, you feel a hand slip around your waist. You turn with a cry of protest on your lips… "No!"

"Yes," he says, "I'm here."

You find yourself gazing into the smiling, teasing eyes of the man you love. He pulls you close; he's relaxed, happy, engorged with his own anticipation.

"You look incredible…" he breathed in deeply. He kisses your lips, then moves down to your throat.

"Come," you say, grabbing his hand.

You rush through the lush green gardens. The scent of plumeria wafts in the air.

You arrive at the door of your garden suite, overlooking the ocean. The sunset casts a golden glow in the room. Your lover picks you up and carries you over the threshold. You kiss him passionately, tasting the salt on his lips. Your passion is urgent and strong. He carries you to the bed; you rip off his shirt, as he pulls off your sarong.

"You are so incredibly beautiful," he whispers as he kisses your neck and moves slowly down.

The whispering revolving fan blades cool your body, but inside, you're on fire. You urgently respond to his body wanting yours. Your lover moves rhythmically to the sound of each wave crashing on the nearby ocean shore. Desire mounting, you move closer to ecstasy.

Fill in the rest of the story…remembering every detail, for *you* are going to re-create this moment in time in your very own bedroom.

Get ready for Paradise!

YOUR OWN TROPICAL PARADISE:
THE SENSUAL ELEMENTS

Is there any place more relaxing than a tropical island? Sun-kissed days are spent in lazy repose by the ocean. Palm trees stir in the Trade Winds, kissing your skin with a cooling breeze. Beads of sweat and coconut scented lotion illuminate your body. The rhythm of the ocean lulls you into a state of bliss, unlike any other. Love abounds on these tropical island retreats...let's bring it home, into *your paradise*...your own master suite.

First get in touch with your most pleasurable experience, memory, or perhaps someplace you've always dreamed of visiting. Search the travel magazines to get a feel for the tropical retreat you want to create.

Describe in full sensory detail the environment you desire, equating it with a fantasy experience you might dream of having.

Did you know...women (or men) who read romance novels have better love lives? Not surprising, since the greatest sex organ in humans is the brain...sorry guys!

Revealing the body is important to this fantasy. It's time to fall in love with your body. Love the body you have and seek health and wellness in every aspect of your life.

One couple we know made a commitment to a wonderful lifetime nutritional adventure that helped them release unwanted inches and gave them energy and a sense of well-being. They found themselves strongly attracted to each other, with passion as alive as it was when they first met.

Bodies...all of us have them! It's vital we do everything in our power to feel as physically good as we possibly can. Our bodies are the lenses through which we see and experience our world. Everything is influenced by how we feel in our bodies. When you have a throbbing headache, it's difficult to not see everything through that pain, that veil of grayness and discomfort, or even depression. When your body is healthy and you feel clean, strong, and vital, the whole world feels alive and full of possibility! You can do anything, conquer anything, imagine and create anything!

For ideas about re-energizing your physical health and increasing your passion, visit **www.PassionByDesign.com**, and click on the Passion Nutrition page.

Tropical retreats embrace the senses with fragrant flowers, the fresh smell of the ocean, stunning sunsets, the sound of the waves and palm fronds whistling from the trade winds.

Delicious island drinks and ripe, mouth-watering fruits make the taste buds whimper with delight. The landscape, the colors, the vibrant movement of nature, is all an exciting starting point, a blueprint waiting to be created in your own romantic tropical island retreat.

Listen! Do you hear it? The sound of the conch shell being blown to announce the beautiful island setting yet to come!

DESIGN AND PURCHASE

The Setting: Lush, languid, revealing, and sensual, this room is filled with fantasy possibilities! Natural wonders abound in the tropics. Verdant jungles, steamy and moist, cascading waterfalls, whispering palms, and fiery volcanoes all transport you and your lover to the perfect retreat.

Nature: earth, sea, and sky. This tropical wonderland offers up one surprise after another. Let nature be your guide in creating your paradise.

With the popularity of import stores, creating this room is at your fingertips *without* draining your vacation fund.

Sight: The color palette is cool and refreshing. It is composed of:
* pearly whites
* soft creams
* sunshine yellows
* bright fuchsia
* aqua
* deep blue
* plumeria pink
* palm frond green

Smell: Yummy delicious smells of coconut, citrus, mango, and coco butter. The fresh leis are made from plumeria blossoms. Flowers are everywhere in tropical settings: floating lotus blossoms, bamboo, plumeria. The scents of the ocean are cool and refreshing, with a hint of clean saltiness. Incorporate these scents into your candles, your florals, your bath products, lotions and perfumes.

Touch: The fabrics in this bedroom should be natural fabrics. Look for pure cotton and linen. Choose sheets with a high thread count for maximum comfort. These are crisp and cool to the touch, perfectly suited to sweltering island nights.

Floors are smooth, polished and cool. They can be wood or stone and topped with rugs that are made of woven materials. You can find these in import shops everywhere. Some natural fibers can be rough on the feet (and the body!) so be sure to check the feel of it with your bare toes. Window treatments should blow in the breeze. They should be light and filmy. Gauze fabrics are always suitable for the tropical island romance, but they are also see-through. Pull down shades can be added to offer privacy, if needed. Another treatment could be dark stained plantation shutters framing the window, providing coolness and shade for your afternoon delight.

Taste: Gather baskets of fresh tropical fruits for bath and bedside. Slivers of fresh coconut can float in your bath, slices of mango and papaya spritzed with slivers of lime. Enjoy tropical umbrella drinks: Mai Tais, Pina Coladas, Mango and Banana Smoothies. You can buy the umbrellas at party stores! Feed your lover slivers of pineapple while bathing in a huge bath of ocean-scented bubbles.

Sounds: Think of the sounds of the ocean, the spray of the waves, the palm trees rustling in the wind. Music is available with all of these natural sounds to flood your retreat with the feelings of being right on your own tropical island!

Tropical music celebrates mother earth. From Hawaii, Tahiti, Jamaica, South America...just think of the island drums and wind instruments. Enjoy sensual singers like Marc Anthony, the Brothers Cazimero, Kui Lee and the ever haunting, soulful voice of Iz: Israel Kamakawiwo'ole.

Water features and fountains are a must for this fantasy room. Hearing the trickling of water is soothing and sensual. Float a beautiful lotus blossom in the fountain. You might want to turn off the water feature at night. It may make a difference in the number of times you have to visit the bathroom!

The Passion Sense: Your body is key in this romantic ambience. Your body is a gift, a beautiful gift, no matter what shape, size or color it is in this moment. Know that you have the power to influence your body toward more health, more vitality, and more energy.

More energy means doing the things you really love to do…you know what we mean! Celebrate; no matter what your stature or size, you will gain great joy in finding your sensual connection to your body (and booty!). Love your body and know you are beautiful and blessed. Start by stroking coconut-scented lotion on your skin. Feel it: soft and supple, isn't it? That's what *he* will love to touch.

Let your hair be loose and tousled, as though the island breeze has found its way into your room. Use Tropical scented shampoo and conditioner. His passion will ignite with the first breeze of scent!

The Elements: Paint your walls a softly gleaming white, reminiscent of white sandy beaches. Strew soft Grass mats on your deep, rich dark wood floor. Check the feel, or the "hand" of the mat before you purchase. Some jutes or sisals can be rough on your bare feet…or body (if the heat of passion pulls you to the floor (your beach). If tile is your preference, think of large squares (at least 18 inches) that reflect the creamy color of the beach.

Paint your bed white. There are many variations of white. There are crisp, clean, clear whites, reminiscent of high, puffy clouds, or a warm white, reminiscent of foam floating on top of a wave. Softer sandy whites can be used effectively. When blending whites, be aware that when placing some clean whites next to softer whites, it can make the softer white look dirty or gray. We're going for romance, here, so stay away from stark white.

Passion Tip:
Buy small pints of paint and paint pieces of poster board. Hang them in the room and view them several times a day when the light changes. Select the paint that is pleasing *most* of the time.

Pair these whites with bed coverings and fabrics in shades of blues that reflect the ocean. These can be:
- dark lapis lazuli blue
- light turquoise
- aqua
- azure blue

This is a very "natural" ambience you're creating. Any color that you see in nature is appropriate for this palette. Choose as your reference:

- the ocean
- the sky
- the white (or even black like lava) sandy beaches
- the bright punches of color in tropical flowers or birds

Be daring! Float your bed in the middle of the room! Try it angled in a corner! Try different angles to see what works, without blocking your walking pattern. This is often done in tropical climates to increase the air circulation. Your headboard can be the backdrop for a bookcase, desk, or loveseat... a perfect place for a sitting area.

Group a couple of chairs and a small table, thus creating a place where you can enjoy the pleasures of a good book, perhaps a romance novel! Here, the two of you can sit and share a quiet conversation, sitting in his lap, to the backdrop of your favorite music.

Hang mosquito-netting overhead. The "ready made" bamboo circles with attached netting can be found in import stores. They simply require hanging overhead with a ceiling hook.

Purchase: In the warm summer months, a comforter is usually unnecessary. Take advantage of the beauty of cotton sheets. If you must use a blanket, buy a sheet for underneath the blanket, and one to cover the top of the blanket, like a bedspread. Hotels in tropical setting do this. It feels cool and crisp. The sheets might be aqua or deep blue. It is the ocean of desire in your room! Buy lots of pillows and use different pastel colored pillowcases within our tropical color scheme.

You can buy inexpensive tropical print fabric or fabric in a solid color from the list above. Remember...nature is the perfect color coordinator. If you see it together in nature, you can't go wrong in this tropical environment. Here's a big decorating tip: many drapery specialists use the glue gun for hemming! You can hem the fabric with the glue gun or a sewing machine. Hang the fabric over your nightstands or use it as a dresser scarf.

Small potted ferns are lovely on the top of dressers and nightstands to bring the "outside nature" in. Buy several inexpensive tall palms and group them together in the corners of your room or just behind the head of your bed that is floating in the middle of the room. Set the potted ferns in decorative baskets, lined with a heavy-duty trash bag or a pot saucer to collect any stray water. Scrunch up some newspaper and surround the pot like a ledge between the edge of the pot and the basket. Some packaged moss from the craft stores can be stuffed on top of the newspaper and around the plant to hide the dirt and the plastic pot. Another decorator trick is to buy some small decorative green plants in four-inch pots. Put each one in deep plant saucer and surround the palm with them. Fill in the empty spaces with green moss. Pose them in a collection as a lush growth in the corners of your room, on top of dressers, and at the ends of your bed.

You might consider purchasing some natural wicker furniture. It is inexpensive and looks great in our tropical environment. If you have a sitting area, buy the wicker chairs or rockers with the large fan backs. Purchase cushions to fit and bring added comfort, and go bold with a deep hue of green or fuchsia! Place a wicker chest at the end of your bed.

Place glass bowls of water on top of the chest and float gardenias from your garden. Also, purchase a tranquil water feature or indoor fountain, perhaps one that has a bamboo spout. Gardening departments of home improvement stores, as well as online catalogues are good sources for indoor fountains. Trickling water is serene and sensual and sets the mood for love.

"Serenity" is just around the corner of "desire on fire!"

Lighting: Invest in a ceiling fan and light combination. To go along with your island theme, try one that has the palm or reed paddles. The price of ceiling fans has dropped dramatically in the last few years, and usually just requires removing your existing overhead light, and replacing it with the fan. Check with an electrician to see if this is possible. It's important to also have a dimmer switch installed.

Of course use lots and lots of tropical scented candles clustered in bamboo trays around the bedroom and bathroom.

Passion Tip:
Use soft pink light bulbs. It casts a warm glow on the room, like a pink sunset over the Hawaiian shores.

Decorate Yourself: Now for decorating yourself…very simple. Sarongs can be found practically anywhere during the summer months…surf shops, drug stores, even the shopping carts inside the malls. They are inexpensive and look good on all shapes and sizes. Ask the sales person at one of the carts to show you how to tie them.

Think of the exotic Hawaiian women at a Luau. They move their bodies sensually whether they are 110 pounds or 210 pounds! It's all in attitude. Picture yourself as the voluptuous Hawaiian dancer: exotic, irresistible, on fire with passion, and chances are, your lover will feel the heat.

ALOHA...you have created your own tropical paradise within a reasonable budget!

Your Passion Notes

PARIS, THE CITY OF LOVE…OOH LA LA

"Were it not for imagination, sir, a man would be as happy in the arms of a chambermaid as of a duchess."

-Dr. Samuel Johnson

CHAPTER TWENTY-NINE
Paris, The City Of Love...Ooh La La

How delightfully sexy you feel as you stroll along the Seine, alive with the thrill of being in the city of love...Paris.

You see brightly colored paintings stretched out across the quay. You walk past artists displaying their life's passion on canvas. You stop in front of a magnificent life size work of art, your breath catching in your throat. It's a luminescent nude sprawled sensually across a chaise longe, gossamer fabric drapes the woman's long legs, falling gently across her breasts revealing one rosy nipple. Her face speaks desire. It's in her eyes and the way she gazes out at the viewer. The woman is *you*. It's your face, your hair, your eyes. You feel exposed, vulnerable, yet excited.

You sense someone looking at you, admiring, undressing, and silently caressing you. Self consciously, you turn to face the artist who painted and exposed *you* on canvas.

He smiles slightly, and without a word, turns back to his painting. You notice his long fingers deftly wielding a paintbrush and your mind races over what those fingers could be doing to you. You attempt a conversation, but your French suddenly escapes you.

"Monsieur, c'est moi!" He doesn't understand what you are trying to convey. Does he not see that he has painted *you*...exposed your desire on canvas. He clearly doesn't understand what you're saying, but his eyes speak the universal language of love.

He motions for you to follow him. In a daze, you find yourself crossing the Pont Neuf to a quiet, tree-lined street on the Right Bank. The carved doors of his apartment open to a grand entry lined with wood paneled walls. You can't help but notice the elaborate silk brocade window treatments and his genuine Louis

XV console table. He's obviously very good at what he does! You're shocked to find yourself in his apartment, wanting to make love with a stranger.

The room is sprawling with sensual and erotic canvases of semi-clad women. Suddenly…he speaks your language (after all…this *is* a fantasy)! He says he sees your body as perfection and has painted you from his dreams.

As he removes your clothes, he strokes your bare skin with his sable brush. With each stroke he commits your body to his memory to be transferred onto his next canvas.

He caresses your neck, between your breasts, down your stomach to your thighs. Your body responds by pressing against him. He kisses your mouth gently; pulling off his shirt, then unbuttons each button slowly, appreciating each new exposure of your skin. He adeptly releases your breasts from your new French lace bra. They are warm as he kisses and nibbles his way downward…

He's on fire with passion. You pull away and suddenly *you* become the temptress. You unbuckle his pants. You kiss him hungrily, moving your mouth slowly down his muscular body. You find the rhythm of love as though you had been together in another lifetime. Your bodies move sensually in the perfect dance of lovemaking. With each breath you reach a new height of ecstasy and it goes on and on…until you reach that perfect culmination of what you've been seeking your entire life.

You fall away from each other, but still caressing fingertips, as you catch your breath. You feel so good, so complete. You suddenly become a little self-conscience and reach for his crisp white shirt. You wrap yourself in it, and walk toward the large French windows overlooking the Seine.

"Champagne?" he inquires softly.

"Oui," you respond. A chilled bottle of Champagne sits beside the bed in a silver bucket of crushed ice, and beside the champagne flutes is a small bowl of fresh ripe strawberries. It's as though he expected you all along.

He pops the cork and slowly pours it into the glasses. You reach for a strawberry, ripe and juicy, and put it to his lips. You both bite it slowly, gazing into each other's eyes, savoring the perfection as the sweet juices caress your tongues…

Keep fantasizing and suddenly your fantasy becomes a reality when you picture your <u>own</u> partner being that sexy French artist….continue with your fantasy and your pleasure!

YOUR OWN PARIS
THE SENSUAL ELEMENTS

What is it about Paris? Ask anyone: which city most represents romance? Paris will be the first city that comes to mind. The French have cultivated romance down through the centuries. Visit the city, and you can't help but be inspired.

The magic that the French have discovered is:
THEY LIVE LIFE FULLY THROUGH THEIR SENSES.

Even their language requires a pursing of the lips, just ready for a kiss at the drop of a baguette!

Every café, every street corner, every shop window, every museum, is a sensual inspiration. Young people are exposed to this input on a daily basis, laying the foundation for a life of sensuality. Once those senses are awakened, one never sees life quite the same. This includes all the faculties: sight, hearing, smell, taste, and touch.

Food is always fresh and displayed as a work of art…a sight to behold! Each meal is a celebrated event, toasted with fine wine. Fresh baked bread and its wonderful aroma, is a mainstay. The French would never consider eating bread that is petrified in a plastic bag for days on end.

A sense of style slips into every aspect of their lives. It seems as though French women are *born* knowing how to dress. They know how to use color, design, and current fashion trends to their advantage. They learn to buy one new piece per season and create personal and unique combinations from existing pieces to update their wardrobe.

French Women choose their wardrobe by quality over quantity. They invest in one timeless, Chanel jacket, rather than numerous trendy pieces that last a mere one or two seasons.

If money is an issue, they learn to shop the resale stores, and find inspiration by strolling the streets and window-shopping, or frequenting the Paris runways. They innately know that a just a peek of cleavage or exposing just a bit of leg, is more exciting than "letting it all hang out," as is so often seen in current fashion magazines. They know sensuality is awakened by a suggestion to the mind, not blatant exposure.

The senses are constantly stimulated with color and beauty, with fragrant gardens, starry skies and romance in the air! It's no wonder that so many fine artists developed their talents in France!

Love is everywhere! It is quite normal to see lovers, strolling arm in arm, or kissing passionately at a street corner. It's the suggestion of love that is infectious!

Bring Paris home. Indulge in the delights of the City of Love.

DESIGN AND PURCHASE

The Setting: The look that defines French Style is firmly anchored in the past, yet thoroughly updated. French style holds a unique pride of place in the world of style and fashion. It's based upon combining, blending, mixing, and enhancing. It utilizes that certain *je ne sais quoi*...that certain ineffable style that's so inherently French.

Salvaged decorative treasures, faience (pottery), candelabras, zinc objects, urns, plaster busts, and books with covers softened and faded with age. These and other *objets trouvé* (found objects) are the style hallmarks.

French style is nostalgia for a time that has passed. It's a lifestyle based in romance that has never, and, hopefully, never will truly vanish.

The bedroom has held a special place throughout French Royal History. The king received visitors here. It was normal for him to conduct business from his bed! There were actually publicly attended ceremonies known as the *levenment* and the *couchment*, where the king's rising and retiring were publicly shared! Needless to say, the king did not particularly want all of his bedtime activities on display as public events!

Sight: Walls and fabrics should be soft tints (sometimes called pastels) of greens, blues, pinks, golds, creams, and ivories. This color palette creates the "signature" of your Paris Chic bedroom. Gold! Gold! Gold! A French interior can't ever have too much gold.

The lines of the furnishings can be either softly curved (Louis XV) or straightened and simplified (Louis XVI) depending on your taste. The more curves, the more feminine...straighter lines, more masculine!

What does this mean for our French bedroom? The furniture is either painted or stained wood. Beds can be upholstered in glazed cotton fabric or linen perhaps with a fleurs de lis pattern or Pierre Deux pattern. Look them up online to peruse fabrics or visit your local retailer. A designer will have extensive resources available.

Choose nightstands that don't necessarily match. They can be painted or stained and accented with gilding (gold). Hardware will typically have an aged patina (finish) and often will be in leaf or floral styles.

Chairs are soft and comfortable and easy to sink into with a good book and a glass of chardonnay while awaiting your lover's arrival.

Smell: For centuries, the French have been renowned for their classic perfumes. Think about Chanel No. 5! The French have claimed credit for creating perfume 500 years ago for the sophisticated court of King François I yet there is documented evidence that perfumed oils existed in Egypt during Cleopatra's lifetime, according to Edith Kunz who wrote the book *"Fatale, How French Women Do It."*

For the sensual smells of this room, consider rose petals, jasmine, and orange blossoms. Layering the smells is imperative for the most lingering pleasures. Start with the bath, then lotions, then perfumes. Put vases and bowls full of cut roses from your garden (every yard should have several rose bushes...after all, they *are* the flower of romance!).

Touch: The fabrics, here, are key to the *touch* experience. The mix of French style is in blending textures and textiles, the well-worn weave of Turkish carpets, faded tapestries, fine cashmeres, brocades, velvets, and plain white cottons.

Look for fabrics at antique stores and vintage shops, or online. A plain velvet or simple cotton bedspread can be dressed up by draping it with a piece of vintage fabric (hem the edges with a beautiful piece of antique lace trim). Accent the bed with pillows in complementary fabrics.

Taste: Bubbles...lots of them in a tall chilled bottle of French Champagne...perhaps Veuve Cliquot. Drop red raspberries into the bottom of your champagne flute. Have a small silver tray of Chocolate Truffles beside the bed for that afterglow.

If you're doing our nutritional program (www.PassionByDesign.com, Passion Nutrition) feed your lover the "Happy Chocolates!"

Sounds: If you remember the 1966 classic French film, *A Man and A Woman* starring Anouk Aimée and Jean-Louis Trintignant, you'll recall it was one of the most sensual and intensely romantic films ever. The soundtrack is a wonderful mix, and should be included in your French Boudoir collection. A very sexy young singer in France today is Alizee. Look for her records online through Amazon. com or other online music vendors. If French jazz is your fancy, look for Stéphane Grapelle. For opera, try Pauline Garcia-Viardot.

Don't forget the sounds of the Seine River! You'll want a quiet fountain for background to your perfect French encounter!

The Passion Sense: French Women are seductresses. They have learned the art of passion by incorporating all of the senses. Re-read our chapter on the Art of Flirting. It says it all!

♥

Even during lovemaking, the French say that one must wear a bit of clothing "very little, if you like, but something."
Fatale, How French Women Do It by Edith Kunz

The Elements: To plan your romantic liaison, think about lots of gilt carvings, yards and yards of silks, brocades, and velvets, and armloads of tassels and trims. You can choose rich mahogany finishes with gold accents or a white or ivory finish with gold or silver accents.

For the walls, select a soft ivory as your base coat. You might want to have a professional decorative finish artist create a subtle wall finish, using multiple layers of color, giving the effect of softly aged walls. It's important to have your faux artist design a sample board for your approval. Keep the sample board in your bedroom overnight, to see how the different lights of day and night affect the color.

Remember to include the ceiling! The ceiling is the same square footage as the floor, and yet in this country we tend to ignore the ceiling by painting it white.

Purchase: The frugal French have come up with a clever way to have style within a budget. Learn where your best local flea markets are located (in France it's *Marché des Puces*). Educate yourself: how the flea markets work, who has the best deals, the reputable dealers, the best times to go, etc.

Go to the largest store that carries the best selection of fabrics (often flea markets will have a selection, as well) in fluid silks or brocades that best reflect the French style. Ladies take note: it is absolutely imperative that these fabrics should complement your skin tone because you have every intention of being sprawled naked across the bed, taunting and tempting your lover into a night of passion! The fabrics should also feel good against your bare bottom…and his!

Be aware that certain violets and yellows can make pale skin look sallow and make you resemble the belly of a frog…NOT the look you're after. If you are a creamy maiden, softly tinted rose or dusty peach will arouse his joystick in record time. This fabric will be used for bedding, window treatments, and upholstery.

Heavy and elaborate draperies, laden with fringe and tassels, were designed to provide the "are you impressed"…and "Wow" factor. However, these heavily cloaked beds provided much more…with draperies drawn shut, it provided a cozy spot for a rendezvous with his currently favored mistress.

You may want to treat yourself by hiring a qualified interior designer to create luxurious bedding. It can be difficult to combine just the right fabrics to make the Paris look your own. The designer will need to calculate yardage, complementary fabrics, number of pillows, and bed skirt design. Make your bedspread, comforter, or duvet versatile by designing it as reversible with two different fabrics.

If your budget doesn't allow for a designer, build your ideas from books and magazines, and the local bedding store.

Be aware that a "too perfect," "too made-up" bed can be off-putting or dampening to his ardor. Leave the duvet cover drawn back invitingly, as if to say… "I'm ready when you are!"

Most guys do not like masses of pillows. Try educating him to the joys of having numerous pillows…teach him that pillows can be used to elevate your hips and other body parts to enhance lovemaking…perhaps he'd change his mind!

A slightly crumpled look sends the message that your bedroom has been a sex playground, and recess is just moments away. When you're focused on lovemaking and make it easily available, whether it's sexy panties or the unmade bed, you remove the physical and mental roadblocks to a frequent and satisfying sex life.

Assorted unmatched painted furniture, occasional pieces in painted creams and ivories with ormolu (gilded bronze) details are hallmarks of Parisian style. Auctions are literally a treasure trove for the French look.

The French are known for their desire to have variety in their love making...even to the point of designing furniture to accommodate creativity and variety.

An extremely high price was recently paid at an auction in Paris for a very unique chair made in the 18th century. It had arms, which moved in and out, a backrest, a seat that would move up and down, and a footrest that pivoted outward. All of the physical gyrations made possible by this amazing chair, encouraged exploitation of the different positions the human body could possibly achieve in sexual satisfaction. No mere "Missionary Position" for these people!

I doubt that such a contraption is made in modern times...what a pity. Think of other pieces of furniture, which might be available for creative sex.

Consider a classic, a very simple upholstered armless chair called the Parsons chair. Have it covered in fabric that complements your Parisian boudoir. The Parsons chair is great for sex! It is a perfect height and width for the man to sit, and the woman to straddle!

Lighting: The *pièce de resistance!* Lighting is the key to bringing mood and beauty into this Parisian room. You can have the most beautiful furniture and accoutrements, but a single overhead ceiling light can completely assault and eradicate the mood you're going for.

Nothing flatters and sparkles more than a glittering crystal chandelier used in an unusual and unexpected location...such as a bedroom. This will usually only work if your ceilings are nine feet or higher. The other possibility would be to find bedside crystal lamps and candelabras or wall sconces.

The crystals dance in the darkness bringing magical light and shadows into the room...it also hides those pesky facial decorations called fine lines... or wrinkles! If you're feeling a little bit handy, you have many choices, here. Home stores have lots of reasonably priced fixtures...lighting stores can offer you even more. You could also comb through flea markets and antique stores for crystals that can be added to your existing fixtures by using a small metal punch and attaching the crystals with fine wire.

Now, the key to making it work is the installation of a dimmer switch. Call an electrician or a handy man. The cost is nominal. If you tend to be a little inhibited, dimming the lights may embolden you to release the wild goddess, smoldering inside!

Candles are a must for enhancing your Parisian experience. Layer lighting by grouping masses of candles on a silver tray.

Designer Tip:
One of something is nice…several (or multiples) of something becomes fabulous!

Decorate Yourself: French women find pleasure in feeling passionate and seductive. Lingerie is an important element to keeping fantasy and romance alive. The French are more comfortable with their bodies, and recognize the importance of being alluring with a little "peek" rather than a bold "reveal." Look online at French lingerie. You'll start to see the importance of bringing a touch of lace, a garter belt with satin trimmed stockings, a lace-up bustier, and matching bras and panties. Indulge…you're worth it, and your man will never question the cost!

"The most beautiful make-up on a woman is passion."
-Yves Saint-Laurent

The Passion Sense: The French Fantasy is all about awakening the romantic *you* by bringing the simple yet elegant style of the French into your home. The French people live a life inspired by art, fresh foods, and glorious gardens. They are savvy and sophisticated. Get yourself ready for this new fantasy by renting French movies, perusing French Vogue, eating French foods, (get out your Julia Child Cookbook!) and walking the gardens near your home. Gather your passion inward and let it come out as you invite your man into your new French Boudoir. Isn't it lovely?

Your Passion Notes

IMMORTAL PASSION

"I would rather have had one breath of her hair, one kiss from her mouth, one touch of her hand, than eternity without it."

- "City of Angels," movie

CHAPTER THIRTY
Immortal Passion

Lightning illuminates the castle courtyard. You run quickly, shielding yourself from the cold night air. You feel a twinge of fear course through your veins.

Rumors of the vampire have surfaced again. The night is dark and aromatic with jasmine in the air. Your arms are laden with the King's garments.

You stifle a sigh of relief as you pass the Royal Guards and enter the King's chamber. Shadows dance around the room from flickering candles mounted on tall candelabras.

The chamber bed is enclosed with draperies that flow to the floor, pooling at the base of the four posts. There is a large rectangular wooden box in the center of the room. It's ornately carved and heavily gilded with flowing bouquets of roses and jasmine trailing down the massive oak sides. A large iron padlock secures the lid. You have always wondered what was inside, but never dared to ask.

Rumors of King Nathaniel's female conquests have circulated throughout the kingdom now and then. As the court's seamstress, you have been in the King's chamber many times, but you have never seen the bed ruffled or undone…and you have never caught the scent of a woman's perfume on his clothing.

There was something about his eyes. Dark and mysterious against his pale white skin. You've always had a secret special love for this man. Hiding on the castle ramparts, you've watched him ride out into the night, cloaked and hooded in his black velvet cape. He always returned before daybreak.

For almost five years, you have sewn and cared for his garments. You've discreetly touched him numerous times while fitting his clothing. Each time, you felt electricity from his body. Alas, he never seemed to notice. However, he did have a way of looking at you that would cause your stomach to quiver. He could see it. He seemed to enjoy the conquest. Was it just a game? You often found yourself dreaming of the possibilities quietly and passionately in your own chamber at night.

"Is that you?" The king's voice penetrated the chamber.

"Yes!" You boldly answer. Your confidence, tonight, is unwavering. He never requested you during the day…it was always in the dark of the night.

King Nathaniel steps toward you. He's alone except for his guards standing at either side of the chamber doors. The king is wearing light gauze undergarments that define his lithe and muscular body. He takes the clothing from your arms. He slips on the pants, then the jacket and turns to face you.

He had commanded that golden threads be sewn into his jacket and pants. He lightly touches the threads you have carefully and lovingly woven.

You kneel to the floor and begin to mark the alterations, beginning with the hem. You gently turn it up and brush his ankle with the palm of your hand. You realize that you've lingered just a little too long and you quickly pull away.

You reach for the inseam of his trousers and as you adjust it you see his royal highness is slightly aroused. You ignore it and continue. You attempt to focus your attention on stitching the golden threads, but his pants are now taut against his groin. You slowly lift your eyes to his.

With a wave of his hand, the king dismisses the courtiers standing at the door.

He reaches for your chin, then gently touches your face. He bends down and begins to kiss you gently. Your hands tremble as you respond to his touch. You try not to feel, but there is no denying his affect on you. He lifts you up and gazes into your eyes. His eyes are dark with passion. He is so incredibly handsome, strong, and virile.

Your king slides his hand down your back and pulls your body against his. You try to pull away from the heat of his fingers, but he only draws you closer. You accidentally prick your finger on the needle you grasp tightly. He plucks the needle from your hand and tosses it aside.

He puts your finger in his mouth and sucks it urgently. He moves to your ear, nibbles it, breathing hard, and then pulls your body closer, molding it into his. He gazes into your eyes. He traces your lips with his finger, moving swiftly, as he lightly brushes his fingers down to your bosom. You can barely stifle the soft groan, which escapes unbidden from your lips.

As his steely black eyes, bore into yours...you feel yourself falling, falling, falling deeply for this man you've coveted afar for so many years. Your lust cannot be denied...nor can his.

"I've always wanted you," he whispers.

He lifts you into his arms and carries you to his bed. He pulls the bedcovers back with a jerk of one hand, never letting go of your body. The sheets are soft and smooth. As though he could read your thoughts, he says. "For you. They've never been slept upon." A question flickers in your mind.

"Where is it that *you* sleep, my Lord? His eyes glance quickly to the box in the center of the room. He doesn't speak. He gazes back into your eyes as he slowly pulls down your blouse and unlaces your corset, string, by string. He kisses your décolleté.

His hands run the entire length of your body. Gently at first, lightly, the touch like a butterfly, steadily, steadily drawing you higher and higher, until you begin to find yourself short of breath, swirling, floating, feeling your ecstasy peak. Your eyes flutter open, and you look into his luminous black eyes. They begin to glow in a shade of red. He opens his mouth arching toward your neck and you realize that *he*, your king, is the vampire.

"I love you," he whispers. "I won't hurt you." Strangely, you are not afraid. His teeth penetrate your neck and you reach the peak of undeniable pleasure that you have never, ever experienced before. He pulls away, just before he turns you immortal...

Let your imagination fill in the rest of the fantasy as you make your man the vampire king, and you are his maiden. His every wish is your command. He is the sexiest man you've ever seen; broad chest, muscled arms, sculpted legs and penetrating eyes...and he is yours.

Wow! Let's cool off a minute and talk "bedroom." It's time to continue our quest to set the stage for our Vampire King and Maiden love haven...

YOUR OWN IMMORTAL PASSION
THE SENSUAL ELEMENTS

Travel with us on an excursion to re-create the English countryside. If the walls of the old English castles could talk, they would reveal centuries of romance, passion, and titillating scandal. It's the reason so many Gothic romance novels use the backdrop of England. It exudes amorous escapades. Let's create some of your own!

The English Bedroom is one that we suggest for winter, where the days are short and the nights are long. England is draped in fantasy...quite literally. The English have an obsession with yards of fabric: draping windows, draping beds, piles of pillows, and luxurious goose down feather beds. All of these things have as much to do with romantic appeal as practical warmth.

The illusion that vampires offer is one of lust and dramatic danger. When they fall in love with those that are not immortal, it raises many questions about the future. Those that fall in love with a vampire want to be "turned" immortal to sustain their love forever after. The vampire typically withholds his desire for blood lust because he wants the woman he loves to live a true mortal life. It is difficult for him to withhold, therefore, it creates delicious tension and unbeliev-able passion and anticipation.

With your Immortal Passion Ambience, you will want to play with the fantasy of titillating seduction. Savor the experience of the romance by letting the tension ebb and flow...like the ocean waves hitting the Cliffs of Dover. Let it last...forever.

Translate this into your English chamber by incorporating layers, layers, layers of fabrics, lighting, clothing that can be removed slowly and seductively. Put a large "vampire chest" at the foot of the bed, under lock and key and fill it with romantic toys, games, and costumes.

English Castles were lit by candlelight, and are key to setting the stage for this ambience. Candles must be watched. Better yet, place them in a shallow bowl of water for added safety. Never leave them burning throughout the night. The passion that you and your lover ignite will keep your love flame burning!

Set the stage for your own fantasies by reading English Romance novels and vampire sagas. Your creative mind will come alive with possibilities.

DESIGN AND PURCHASE
BE THE HEROINE IN YOUR OWN ROMANCE NOVEL

The Setting: Dream of being in your bedchamber tucked into a high-framed bed, under a velvet down comforter with your lover.

A *portière* (a drapery treatment to cover a door) is a wonderful addition to our romantic bedroom. These were used in medieval times to keep out the chill-ing winter drafts. It also creates intimacy, an air of invitation, surprise, a sense of curiosity to see what is behind the curtain. Since it will be seen from both front and back, be sure to make these reversible, so that each side is beautifully finished. When you make a change in your décor this allows you the versatility of simply reversing the hangings.

Sheathe your furniture with tapestry runners in rich colors...and golden threads. There are many available catalogues, retail, and online sources for velvet slipcovers, duvets and coverlets. Select those that feel wonderful to the touch, warm and inviting for bare skin. Your intention is to feel as much of your bare skin next to his as soon as possible!

Sight: Picture a room within a room, which is the way the English used to keep out cold drafts and provide a warm and private love nest. Picture luxurious lacy pillows, complemented with layers of duvets and coverlets, finished with a lacy bed skirt. A designer tip is to layer your antique lace tablecloths spread between the box spring and mattress. Use corded tassels to tie back drapes and curtains.

Smell: The English are known for their incredible gardens. The garden areas are a source of beauty and wonderful smells. Bring roses into your chamber along with lilacs, gardenias, and other fragrant blooms. Float the blooms in crystal or glass bowls of water, or vases. Make certain the floral you choose are pleasing to your King. You can layer the scents with complementary scented candles. Spray rose water in the air. For a completely sensual affair, toss rose petals, lots of them, onto your sheets before making love. (You can collect petals for a week or two and keep them in plastic bags in the refrigerator drawer until ready to use on your night of seduction.) Have you ever rubbed a rose petal on your cheek? It's blissfully soft. That's how good it feels to make love on masses of rose petals. The scent is released into the air and....oh my!

Touch: English bedrooms are laden with florals, chintz, patterns, luxurious down comforters, and loads of pillows. The fabrics are usually large-scale pat terns, florals, in polished or unpolished cotton chintz.

Think English and you think garden. Florals abound from subtle to abundant. Use lots of patterns, repeating one common element such as color or shape.

For example, choose a cream cotton chintz bedspread covering a luxurious down duvet, and layer it with bright blue floral shams, and finish it with bright blue, cream, and apricot decorative pillows. Layers of soft cotton throw rugs cover the dark, smoothly polished walnut floors.

Many men want to make love in places other than the bed. You don't feel comfortable with it for fear that it will ruin, stain, or mess up the furniture. You're missing the point. In fact, this is what it's all about!

Don't miss a great opportunity to have steamy, slippery sex in a place other than the bed. You can cover your chairs with throws, extra lengths of fabric, etc. He will welcome your adventurous spirit, and be happy to hand over his American Express card when he knows that you are focused on **his** pleasure!

As for the male fantasy of having wild, unbridled sex on the bearskin rug, remember that men were originally the hunters. It is intrinsic to their nature to want to hunt, as it is intrinsic to a woman's nature to want to create a warm and comfortable home for herself and her family (we call this shopping therapy!).

Taste: Warmth and comfort along with delectable treats for the senses fulfill the taste fantasies of our English bedroom. For breakfast in bed before or after a romantic interlude, serve a selection of wonderful hot teas accompanied by warm scones, clotted cream and raspberry jam on a silver tray. For those toasty evenings, mulled wine or port along with toasty bread served with room temperature Stilton cheese, warm honey, dried apricots and figs, and walnuts. Keep mints or mint leaves in a small carafe beside the bed for refreshing your palate.

Sounds: Old World Fantasies require Old World music. Think about movie soundtracks you've heard that reflect this era. How about "Rob Roy," "Romeo and Juliet" (the version from 1968), Nothing is more English than the Beatles. If you're an opera fan, look for Paul Potts to download onto your music system. Let the music carry you to your own crescendo!

The Passion Sense: Inspire your romantic fantasies to come alive with researching English Romance Novels. If you don't have time to read, go to the library and check out the books on tape. They are fun, titillating, and will get you in the mood! Rent "Shakespeare in Love" with Gwyneth Paltrow. The passion in that movie is exciting and inspiring! Lots of heaving bosoms in it, as well!

Introduce your romantic bedroom by lacing up your bustier, donning your long robe, and inviting your man to share a goblet of rich red wine. Enjoy the fantasy of you, the maiden, and your man, the King!

Purchase: The English acquire their treasures generation after generation. A carved wooden chair might have come down from a past King or Queen. The family heirlooms are typically a mix of styles, such as Chippendale, Sheraton,

Queen Anne, Jacobean, or Victoria. The colors will most likely be in a softly faded palette, aged through the passing of time.

Choose large-scale patterns, and lots of them! Cabbage roses, florals, anything from nature or the garden will be a good choice.

Look for rich dark wood furniture. Imposing four-poster beds that can be swathed and draped with those yards and yards of fabric. If your room cannot handle a four-poster bed, create a canopy from fabric draped from the ceiling.

Search online or at local antique stores or estate sales for rich, dark wood furniture: Mahogany, walnut, dark oak are some of the possible choices. For the bedroom, look for tall dressers (called highboys). For a nightstand, look again for those dark woods (a marble top would be lovely), but if your budget needs a little trimming, you can select a round table from a home store and cover it with a fabric skirt that puddles on the ground. Underneath you can hide unsightly items like magazines, personal treasures, or even some fantasy love toys!

For the windows, remember that chilly night air. A layer of creamy sheer next to the window to softly filter the light, then layer with side panels of rich drapery fabrics. Wooden, wrought iron, or brass drapery hardware (like rods and rings) are perfect for the English Bedroom.

Heavy, solid and strong, the castle withstands the onslaught of its enemies and the challenge of the English cold winters, as well as the scandalous lives of the royalty!

Lighting: We confront winter darkness with an abundance of candles. The flickering candlelight allows just enough illumination to see the chilly winter frost making patterns on the windowpanes. Choose lighting that flatters you. Banish the ceiling light overhead! Instead, go for English romance, choosing lamp styles in brass, porcelain or silver. (all with dimmer switches). For overhead, choose a crystal chandelier with a dimmer hooked into the wall or remote.

Candles, candles everywhere. Pull out some of your beautiful platters or silver trays that you received as wedding gifts. Large candles can be placed side by side. Put as many on the trays as will fit. Be careful, don't buy too many scented candles or the scents may compete with each other. They cast a soft glow, sculpting your lover's face in a golden light.

Make a ritual of lighting candles. With each wick, you ignite fire, the symbol of passion. You stroke his face…re-igniting and re-confirming the love you share.

When a woman understands that a man's nature is to hunt, she begins to understand that a man needs to be hunting in order to feel like he is a success, that he has a purpose in life, and that he is fulfilling it.

When the hunt is on, he is in his element, master of the universe, king of all he surveys. When he has bagged his prey (translate: gotten married), his raison d'être might begin to diminish just slightly.

You, the woman, have the ability to keep him interested in continuing the hunt with suggestive looks, unexpected actions, and provocative changes in herself, her attitudes and her environment. This keeps him just slightly off balance. It does not allow complacency to set in, and it keeps him keenly interested in continuing his conquest of his chosen mate. And that mate is **you**, for the duration of his life!

Decorate yourself: One constant in English Romance is "the heaving bosom." Battles were fought for it, men in armored suits raised their swords in its honor, and ballrooms were overflowing with the ubiquitous bosom. Look for drawstring bustiers, for they are sexy, and fascinating to a man.

Shawls of velvet are easy to make and feel good next to the skin. Yards of pearls can drape your neck, your heaving bosom, and your stomach. Long robes with velvet cuffs (easily added by your tailor) can keep you warm.

So now you've created a wonderful platform to begin your English Love Affair. Bring him into your chamber now…and let it begin with a Kiss.

Saying "I love you" can become routine. Looking at your handsome man and saying "I'm *so* in love with you" means *so* much more!

Your Passion Notes

HOLLYWOOD GLAM…
LIGHTS, CAMERA, ACTION!

———————————————— ♥ ————————————————

"In a great romance, each person plays a
part the other really likes."

- Elizabeth Ashley, actress

CHAPTER THIRTY-ONE
Hollywood Glam... Lights, Camera, Action!

"A kiss is a lovely trick designed by nature to stop speech when words become superfluous."
-Ingrid Bergman

Remember, in the very beginning of this book we promised you wild, passionate love with Brad Pitt, Hugh Jackman, George Clooney, or whoever else rings your bell? This is your opportunity. It's all about creating your own fantasy around "Hollywood Glam." You and your man are actors starring in your own movie; one filled with drama, passion, and romance...

THE FANTASY

A tingle of nervous anticipation sends shivers down your back as you walk the winding streets of the studio lot. Golf carts whiz by, perhaps holding studio heads with the next great movie about to happen!

You were virtually plucked from obscurity. It is a Hollywood moment every waitress, store clerk, or caterer hopes for: the moment of being discovered. For you, it happened at a small theatre on La Cienega Boulevard. A dozen actors were on the bill, each doing one-act scenes before an audience of studio executives, agents, and casting directors. It was your defining moment. That night, the director of the "next big movie" was looking for an unknown to play the leading lady.

Now, you're actually on the studio lot. You were chosen! Your stomach has butterflies, but your mind has absolutely no doubts about your capabilities as an actor. This is what you've trained for your entire life!

You turn the corner. There it is…Studio A. You see the tall, lean figure of your soon to be leading man crossing the lot ahead of you - his stride long and sure, male and confident. He's more handsome than you ever dreamed!

You exhale deeply. "Get a grip, girl," you admonish yourself. "It's only Brad Pitt (George Clooney, Antonio Banderas, fill in your favorite Hollywood hunk du jour). He doesn't even see you, but you are confident in your prowess and your expertise as an actress to soon make him never forget you. You firmly square your slim shoulders and walk resolutely toward the set.

As you draw near, your mind is spinning, You, yes *you*, have been selected to be the leading lady in the hottest new movie of the year, *The Endless Night*, a lavish, elegantly scripted drama that captured and enchanted your active imagination the first time you read the script.

The door to the set opens. How could it be possible! The set is dressed just as you have envisioned! Old Hollywood glamour beckons you.

Crystal chandeliers, not one, but two, sparkled brightly above the monstrous white bed, dramatically sheathed in white silk satin. Sitting beside the bed, is a white leather chair trimmed with black in the classic Art Deco style that you so love. A bronze of Barishnikov, your childhood idol during your years of ballet lessons, floats effortlessly in his out-stretched arms, head flung back. A plush sheepskin rug covers the floor, where you know from reading the script; you are expected to do your passionate love scene with the incredibly handsome leading man.

Your voice catches in your throat as *he* approaches, but your "hello" is as smooth and sensuous as Lauren Bacall. You feel his emerald eyes sweep your long, slender limbs, firmed and supple from years of working out at the ballet barre. He draws in his breath…he obviously likes what he sees!

He tilts his head; his sensuous lips that you had seen so many times filling the silver screen, part slightly, drawing you near, in spite of yourself. You run your fingers through your long mane of chestnut hair, teasingly. An old childhood habit you can tell that he finds alluring. His subtle reaction encourages your confidence to do this part well.

"You're beautiful," he states boldly.

"Thank you," your eyes sweep the room, "I'm looking forward to working with you."

Your leading man walks to the chilled silver bucket, and lifts out the bottle of La Grand Dame. Your epicurean eye unconsciously scans the label for the vintage, 93, a great year. Your mouth waters slightly in anticipation.

"Champagne should calm the nerves," he says coolly. "Usually we would have had the opportunity to meet and rehearse before this, but our director wants the spontaneity to come from the unfamiliar and forbidden place. Are you okay with that?"

"I'm just fine," you reply with confidence and a flick of your silky hair.

"Beautiful lady…I'm not so sure now that it's *you*, I'm worried about… it's me. You're the most intriguing woman. Where does that certainty come from?"

He looks slightly taken off guard. You've surprised him with your poise and decorum.

"I've always known my destiny," You reply with a quiet smile.

Your leading man studies you, withholding words.

"Quiet on the set", brings you back to awareness of others around you.

"Places, everyone," the assistant director yells.

This is just the beginning!

"On your marks!" The first AD yells.

You look down at the floor to see you are perfectly placed on the "X". You take a steadying breath.

The clapboard snaps. The Director calls, "Action!"

Your leading man grips your shoulders and yells with passion, "What do you want from me? What!" His clear green eyes penetrate yours and you can feel the flutter in your stomach.

You respond to him with the lines you memorized, but now they are yours. "You! You *are* what I want! Only you!"

He looks into your smoldering eyes and pulls you close. You feel his passion and clearly mounting desire…and it's all for you! Your breasts harden, unbidden. You push your body into his. Your lips are swollen with desire and you kiss him, hard and aggressively.

It's almost uncontrollable. He continues to kiss you and caress you, until somewhere in the distance outside your desire, you both finally hear, "Cut… Cut…The director finally has to scream…"CUT!"

You step away from each other and laugh, embarrassed. The crew looks flushed from your heated scene.

Your leading man shivers slightly as he whispers in your ear. "You excite me, beyond words. Will you meet me after we wrap?"

You take a steadying breath. "I'm flattered, but no thank you." You glance across the studio set and see the man you truly love, standing amongst the crew.

He's smiling a knowing smile. He's your man. *He* was the motivation for your scene, and he knows it. The arousal the leading man had felt during the scene came from *you* and the memories of the incredible night of love making you had experienced with your man just hours before dawn.

The actor follows your gaze and smiles regretfully.

"Lucky guy," he says, as he walks over and extends his hand.

You smile into your lover's eyes and know that you've never been more deserving of the title: *"The Sexiest Woman Alive!"*

YOUR OWN HOLLYWOOD GLAM
THE SENSUAL ELEMENTS

Steamy! Let's create your own movie set! Borrow from the glamour of the old movies. Put your lovemaking on center stage and call "Action!" Think of Cary Grant or Marilyn Monroe, who exuded sexuality.

In the movie-making world...anything goes! It's elegant and stylish, romantic and sensual. Every sense is heightened, and larger-than-life on the silver screen.

Lavish use of sparkle, glitter, bling, and glamour...are all elements of our fantasy set. Think of the 40's movies when black and white was the only option. The set designers made abundant use of geometric shapes, shiny and silky fabrics, and metallic finishes along with a refined color palette. Perfect lighting made black and white seem as though it was living color. The sets were elegant and flamboyant.

Nightclubs were a big part of the old Hollywood era: the Rainbow Room, the Stork Room and 21 were among the most popular. One could escape the trials and pressures of daily life dancing the night away to the music of Tommy Dorsey's Big Band.

Pop the champagne, dim the lights, don your satin robe and sit down with your lover to enjoy some great old films: *The Thin Man, Back Street, An Affair to Remember* will inspire you. Extended voyages on ocean liners offered great settings for romantic interludes. The affairs built to a climax over the rolling seas in the decadent luxury of these elegant ships.

Be the director of your own movie!

DESIGN AND PURCHASE
BE THE STAR ON YOUR OWN MOVIE SET

The Setting: Hollywood is about fantasy, excitement, drama, and the ability to put you in the scene. Everything is done for maximum entertainment and to heighten the senses.

Perhaps every young girl has dreamed, at one time or another, of being on the silver screen and seeing her name on the marquis in lights. Imagine walking the red carpet in your designer gown and your ears and neck adorned with thousands of dollars in jewels.

This is your moment to really "glam" it up.

Sight: The colors in this fantasy room are "Old Hollywood." The Palette is composed of:

- oyster whites
- cool blues
- silver
- butter yellow

Paint the walls a muted blue green, accented with shades of oyster around the baseboards. Create faux panels (approximately 4 feet wide by 5 feet high) all the way around the room by using thin strips of molding painted with silver or gilded with silver gilt. Within each of the panels, you can either have a decorative artist paint flowing branches of cherry blossoms or use cut outs of ready made wallpaper, or simply paint the inside of each panel with varying shades of wall color.

Smell: Go back to the classics for this divine and sensuous fantasy. Perfumes were classic: try Chanel #5 or Shalimar.

Fresh flowers are a must, in bundles, everywhere! Perfume the air with gardenias…you might even float a few in a crystal bowl. Remember to keep a light hand here because floral fragrances can get heavy. Always have a few fresh cut flowers; roses are perfect for this, in a small crystal vase on your table. It's part of the fantasy: you received flowers for your magnificent performance as the seductress in your own play. If your lover sees the flowers on your table often enough, he may start buying them for you!

Touch: Select luxurious carpet for the floor in the same family of colors as the walls, a soft blue green. Be sure to specify a thick pad…in anticipation of hot nights of passion, making love on this sea of blue green.

Lighting is everything, darling. The light fixtures should be very clean lined, with finishes in the cool colors of this moonlit palette. Lamps can be pewter or chrome, geometric rather than fussy. Strategically place small halogen lights discretely behind furniture. Use this to create areas of light and dark, a dynamic contrast of floating panels against the softly hued walls.

Get out those incandescent pink light bulbs and pop them in a bedside lamp. Remember how flattering pink tones are to the naked skin. Always be certain to put all lighting on dimmer switches. Attach crystal beads around the arms of a sleek pewter chandelier. Crystals reflect light and create an ambiance of romance, sparking all the possibilities of love.

The bed for this showstopper room is made of padded, quilted satin, resplendent in tones of oyster and pearl. All the furniture and the bedding are tones of iridescent oyster and pearl.

Monogramming was introduced during the Renaissance era, when hand woven linens were emblazoned with a coat of arms identifying the noble family. It was in the 1920's, however, that the design firm of D. Portault, of Paris reintroduced the monogram as an accent to fine linens. It quickly became fashionable, and lends a special touch to our Hollywood Glam boudoir. It is a keynote addition to the bedroom that says, "I Love You," by intertwining your initials with his.

Monogram plush white towels and matching robes. Terry slippers are a great addition to this setting, as well.

For this specific look, bedside tables should be matched pairs. Fully mirrored chest-style nightstands on straight legs would be a perfect choice here. Formal balance and symmetry count in this look.

Draperies are shimmery panels of ivory satin, allowed to puddle luxuriously on the floor.

This is one room where your make-up table should stand out as a work of art. After all...you are the leading lady in this fantasy environment. Drape a simple table with a few yards of silk. Have a glass company cut a mirror, the shape of the top of the dressing table. Beveled edges are best. Use silver cups to hold your make up brushes, and search antique stores for a sterling silver mirror and hairbrush set to display. Use small trays to hold the most beautiful of your perfume bottles.

Purchase a silver hook in an angular shape and hang it on the wall in your bathroom. Buy an ivory colored padded silk hanger and cover the hooked part of the hanger with a few pieces of satin ribbons. Hang your most luxurious lace nightgown on the hanger and display it on the silver hook. If you don't already have a gorgeous piece of lingerie, Victoria's Secret sells seductive pieces at reasonable cost. Go for something in ivory lace, or blush satin (remember to select one that complements your skin tone). It's definitely Hollywood Glam.

Taste: Hollywood Glam is all about luxury, extravagance and sophistication... Enjoy champagne cocktails, caviar on toast points, and strawberries dipped in imported Belgian chocolate. Titillate the taste buds and enjoy these delicacies with your finest crystal goblets and china. For caviar, always use a non-metallic spoon as it changes the flavor. We recommend a mother of pearl. Enjoy!

Sounds: Let's talk soundtrack. Music is a natural for this "set." How about the bluesy voice of Louis Armstrong or Nat King Cole? Allow their voices to audibly caress you and your lover.

Look around....you are on the set of your own movie. See your name and your lover's on the marquis in bright lights. Drift off into the world of glam... and love.

The Passion Sense: Movies are all about drama and fantasy. Make your romance over-the-moon exciting by being a character in a movie. Cast off inhibitions and become the star that you are! Your leading man will welcome you into his arms and bring your fantasy of Hollywood Glam to a climax! Enjoy being a star...you deserve it!

Decorate yourself: Gowns...gowns...gowns. Not ballroom, but silky, slinky lingerie that enhances your curves and swings the pendulum from a sleeping gown to a passionate gown. Look in Victoria's Secret or other lingerie specialty shops for these sensuous gowns. Try bright red satin, and compliment it with bright red lip stain (you don't want your kissing to leave red all over his face so stain is better than lipstick!). Don't forget a silk robe. It's a must in our setting. Watch old 40's movies and you will always see the star in a seductive silk robe with the tie wrapping her waist. One tug, and it falls open to reveal your beautiful body. (Yes, your body is absolutely beautiful, no question, for you are the star of this fantasy).

Costume jewelry is a must (or the real thing if you have it)-lots of dangly rhinestone or diamond earrings, delicate choker necklaces, or maybe even strands and strands of pearls. More is better. This makes foreplay even more passionate as he removes your jewels one by one.

Hair should be tousled and playful. If you have long hair, maybe twirl it up in a single barrette so that when released, your hair cascades down around your neck.

High heels...absolutely! Higher is better! Even if they are uncomfortable, you're not wearing them for long. Just do it! Buy a garter belt with stockings.... men love these! Make love with your garter belt on, and have him slowly release and remove each stocking while you moan with desire.

Your Passion Notes

CELEBRATE, CELEBRATE, CELEBRATE!

♥

"Love doesn't make the world go round,
love is what makes the ride worthwhile."

-Elizabeth Browning, author

CHAPTER THIRTY-TWO
Celebrate, Celebrate, Celebrate!

You have just awakened the fire that will sustain your relationship. Watch how the awakening of your senses spills over into every aspect of your life! Passion is infectious!

You have fallen in love anew. Your lover is now your partner in living an exquisite life. You are happier, and so is he. Passion is now your muse. Never again will you be content to passively exist in your surroundings. You will now live it, breathe it, harken it to contribute a quality of life that will bring harmony and balance.

Your family relationships and friendships will be stronger, your work will be more productive, you'll have more money, and your play will be more fulfilling! Visualizing all of this gives you the power toward making it happen!

Your life will intensify with an energy that cannot be denied. You walk with a light that illuminates from your soul. You invite change as your matchstick to set the world aglow!

You have realized the importance of your surroundings in setting the stage for your life. You will appreciate, from this point forward, the role that beauty plays in enhancing the quality and joy of living.

When you feel yourself falling into the abyss of routine…throw yourself a lifeline and re-work the steps. Refresh yourself with the Passion Quiz. You may have new answers, and you certainly have created new memories since your Passion Journey began. Re-evaluate your surroundings. Don't despair…change is good! You're just waking up to another chapter of your life!

Remember…Change is inevitable and it is good. The need for it says we are alive!

We're here for you. Visit us on our website: **www.PassionByDesign.com.** You'll find pictures, ideas, fun downloads, and lots of support for your new passionate life!

Being a passionate person means living a passionate life. Set out on the adventure with your lover today and *every* day. You'll never turn back once you've lived the life of…

Passion By Design!

Your Passion Notes

ABOUT THE AUTHORS

Paula McChesney, ASID, CID

Paula McChesney, ASID (American Society of Interior Designers), CID (Certified Interior Designer) is the President and CEO of McChesney Design Studio, Inc. and Passion by Design™. She founded her original company, Color Concepts in San Francisco, specializing in personal style color analysis.

Winner of numerous design awards, Paula brings a broad international vision to her field as she creates her design work throughout North America, Mexico, New Zealand and Hawaii. McChesney Design Studio provides residential interior design services to an exclusive clientele. Her experience also includes yacht interior design; television set design, as well as the creation of a custom line of furnishings, fragrance and bedding that are currently under development.

She has participated in a variety of television and radio shows, as well as contributed her services to more than 15 designer showcase homes. Paula was the President of the prestigious American Society of Interior Designers, (ASID) California Peninsula chapter in 2009.

Paula has been widely published and is a sought after public speaker and educator. She lives in Carmel Valley, California, with the love of her life, Brooks McChesney, and their Dalmatian, Chassagne Montrachet.

Sandy Peckinpah

Sandy Peckinpah was inspired to write her first book, *Rosey the Imperfect Angel,* after the birth of her daughter, Julianne. The fairy tale for children with special needs was published and immediately caught the attention of news media throughout the country. Sandy and her daughter toured the country to appear on numerous national television talk shows, news shows, radio programs, as well as newspaper interviews, and speaking engagements throughout the U.S. Her second book, *Chester the Imperfect All Star*, followed. The books went on to be used by hospitals, clinics, and special needs charities.

In addition to writing, Sandy worked in the television industry as an actress, participating in television movies and series and worked with her late husband, David Peckinpah, (Yes, everyone always asks...Sam Peckinpah was his uncle). David was the executive producer and writer of numerous television series: *Sliders, Beauty and the Beast, Silk Stalkings*, among others.

She returns to her passion for writing in her collaboration with her life long friend, Paula McChesney, to create and write *Passion by Design*. Sandy focuses on projects that make a difference in people's lives. Her fairy tales bring enlightenment, wonderment, hope, and joy. *Passion By Design* is one more opportunity to do just that!

Sandy lives in Southern California with her children, (Trevor, Julianne, and Jackson), her extended family, friends, and pets.

What is ASID...

ASID (American Society of Interior Designers) was founded in 1975, and is the oldest, largest, and most prestigious professional organization for interior designers.

Professional members of ASID must pass rigorous acceptance standards: they must have a combination of accredited design education and/or full-time work experience and pass a two-day accreditation examination administered by the National Council for Interior Design Qualification (NCIDQ).

ASID is a community of people driven by a common love for design, and committed to the belief that interior design, as a service to people, is a powerful, multi-faceted profession that positively changes people's lives.

To book speaking engagements for your association or organization, contact us at our e-mail address: info@PassionByDesign.com

Made in the USA
Charleston, SC
18 February 2011